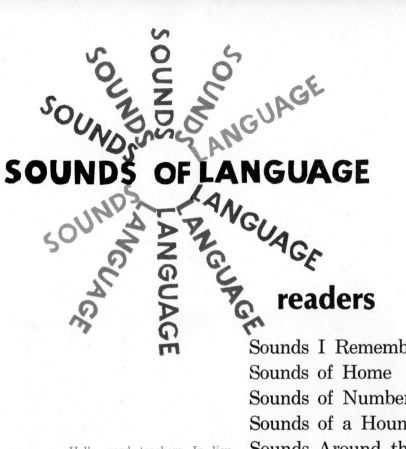

SOUNDS OF LANGUAGE

readers

Hello, good teachers. In lieu of talking with you face-to-face, we are relying on man's miraculous invention, print. These annotations, like this reader, are an invitation for all of us to rejoice in the act of language and how it influences man's becoming.

Holt, Rinehart and Winston, Inc.
New York Toronto London Sydney

SOUNDS OF A HOUND DOG

This title is not to be taught as five separate words. It is a unified sound with its special meaning. To prepare children for reading it themselves, you begin by reading the title aloud (several times, if necessary) with warm and natural intonation, inviting the children to chime in as the sounds become familiar. Thus, children are talking their way to reading.

BY BILL MARTIN JR.
IN COLLABOR-ATION WITH PEGGY BROGAN

TEACHER'S EDITION
PRIMER

Cassette recordings of Bill Martin's readings and interpretations and skillbuilding activities are now available with the *Sounds of Language* program. He is assisted in the recordings by the renowned guitarist, Al Caiola, who weaves musical underpinnings to the language, and by Noodles, a little ghost who represents a child's point of view. The purpose of the recordings is to add enjoyment and enlightenment to the reading process.

This book is dedicated
to my friend and colleague
LUTIE CHILES
whose work in elementary education
at William Jewell College
is an enduring monument.

Children may be interested in knowing why an acknowledgment section appears in a book. It's a legal obligation to show that permission was granted for reprinting a copyrighted selection in keeping with the copyright law.

ACKNOWLEDGMENTS

The authors and Holt, Rinehart and Winston, Inc., thank the following authors, publishers, agents and parties whose help and permissions to reprint materials have made this book possible. If any errors in acknowledgments have occurred, the errors were inadvertent and will be corrected in subsequent editions as they are realized.

Thomas Y. Crowell Company, Inc., for "Who Did?" from DID YOU FEED MY COW? Compiled by Margaret Taylor. Copyright © 1956 by Margaret Taylor. Used by permission.

Friede Orleans Joffe, for permission to reprint Ilo Orleans' poem, "Frog on the Log."

Patricia K. Miller and Iran L. Seligman, for permission to use an adaptation of their story and illustrations, "At Home on the Ice."

Punch Publications, Ltd., London, for permission to use the painting by Amy Murray on page 160.

G. Schirmer, Inc. and Chappell & Co., Inc., for "I FEEL PRETTY," music by Leonard Bernstein and lyrics by Stephen Sondheim. Copyright © 1957, 1959 by Leonard Bernstein and Stephen Sondheim. All rights reserved. Used by permission.

Schroder Music Company (ASCAP), Berkeley, California for "EVERYBODY SAYS," words and music by Malvina Reynolds. Copyright © 1957 by Schroder Music Company. All rights reserved. Used by permission.

Acknowledgment is made to Betty Jean Martin, for permission to use her character, Noodles.

Acknowledgment is made to our permissions editor, William Bostock, to Whit Brogan for helpful library research, to Judy Kopecky for keeping the financial and statistical procedures in hand.

And no acknowledgment list would be complete without special thanks and appreciation to Lydia Vita and Mel Rohr for their skilled preparation of this book for delivery to the printer.

Other acknowledgments appear with materials used.

You may be wondering about our system for annotating this book. Actually, we have tried to make the kinds of markings we think you would make as you read the essay and plan ways for making the stories and poems most enjoyable and useful for yourself and the children. Our markings are by no means complete. They are a starter, and we hope you will take pen in hand and continue the kinds of annotations that work best for you.

CONTENTS

The SOUNDS OF LANGUAGE program is designed to enhance a child's use of language as a speaker, a listener, a writer and a reader, and to give you teachers both the opportunities and the skills for bringing dimensions into the teaching of reading that conventional programs have precluded.

Our essay at the back of this book and the page-by-page annotations are not prescriptive. Nor are they ritual. They offer you up-to-date information about language, about human growth and about classroom organization. They offer a view of the classroom as a launching pad to human greatness, both yours and the children's.

The pupil texts are a collection of stories, poems, songs, essays, pictures and paintings that celebrate the human yen for beauty, excitement, drama, well-being and pleasure. Once you have a rich familiarity with your and the children's materials in the SOUNDS OF LANGUAGE program, you will have become, we believe, another link in mankind's attempt to stay the chaos of an increasingly hostile world environment.

We believe you will also discover that, without becoming a slave to a teacher's guide, you can fashion day-by-day language encounters that help children claim their human heritage as successful readers.

SOUNDS OF A HOUND DOG

So here we go into the book. You soon will have enough insights into the program that you will feel comfortable with the page-to-page annotations. You also can depend on your own capabilities in editing and expanding our suggestions to fit the unique needs of a child or a group of children. The strength of this program is in you, in the children, and in the language

potato potato potato potato potato potato

insights found in these materials. Such a combination of talents is sure to succeed. For example, notice how quickly you and the children find the linguistic pattern in this culturally based "reading riddle" and exploit it into a reading skill. In no time at all, children will be following the numbers sequentially even though they are not sequentially aligned.

potato stew,

If you're not
potato mad,
I'll potato you!

potato

potato

potato

potato
more,

potato

A JINGLE,
PICTURE BY KELLY OECHSLI

I am a baby chick.

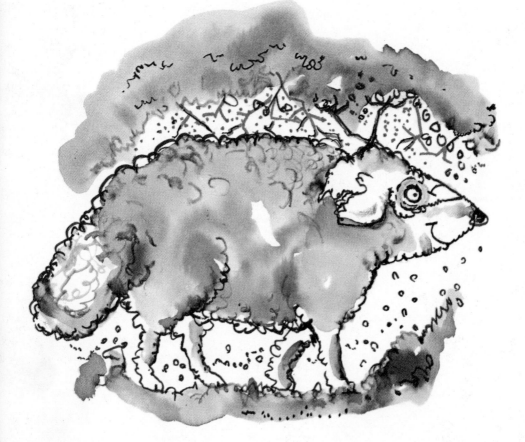

Cheep. Cheep. I Am Not a Sheep.

by Bill Martin Jr. with drawings by Peter Lippman

Watch your children's faces as they look at these opening pages in their new book. The pages were designed to capture the curiosity of the children and to assure them that their long, thoughtful looks will be rewarded. As they figure out the picture puzzles and make observations about the regularity of the rhyming words and other features of the print, they will be building the all-important attitude that is basic to learning to read. They will have the expectation that the pages in books are workable puzzles

I am a little red hen.

Cluck. Cluck. I am not a duck.

with clues and surprises for the person reading. Gradually you can help them extend this attitude to include clues from the literary structure, sentence patterns, spelling patterns of words, and even punctuation. The notion that the author and artist are friendly human beings leaving clues for the person reading, is qualitatively different from the "bogged down" feeling of having to memorize countless rules in order to ever make a go of print.

I am a mother sweeping the floor.

Swish. Swish. I am not a fish.

I am a little brown dog.

Bow-wow-wow. I am not a cow.

Be sure that the children have heard and read and enjoyed their stories and poems before going into any analytical discussions. If you interrupt the reading to make observations about the art or print, the children are denied an esthetic literary experience. They are also kept from depositing the literary structure and sentence patterns in their linguistic storehouses for later use. For a discussion of the importance of this kind of depositing, see TE page 16.

I am a pigeon picking seeds.

Pick. Pick. I am not a chick.

Are you and the children enjoying the playfulness of this story? Great! If the children want to read it "a million times, over and over," be assured they are depositing both language-ways and reading skills that later they'll use and verbalize.

I am a mole digging a hole.

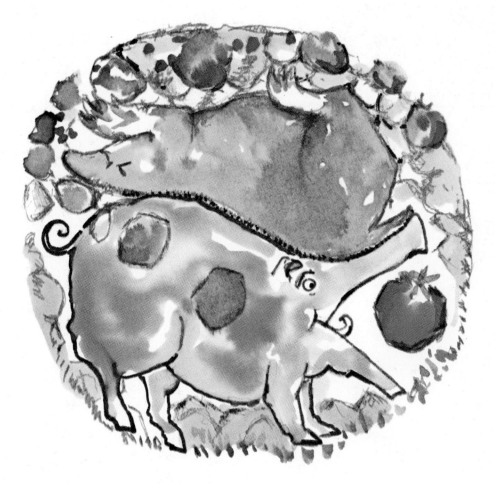

Dig. Dig. I am not a pig.

If you and the children have been enjoying some analytical discussions about these pages, be sure to put the story back together again after each discussion, reading it joyously from beginning to end. Skill-building activities should not decimate or degrade either literature or language.

I am a coyote baying at the moon.

Howl. Howl. I am not an owl.

What fun to have the visual forms of the words look like their meanings! Now if you ask, "What do you see interesting about the words on this page, children?" and some child responds, "I see some words that sure do look noisy," you will have proof that here is a child who knows that there is more to a word than its spelling pattern or its phonic components.

I am Susan and Billy going out the door.

SLAM!
BANG! CLATTER!
ROAR!

I am not a dinosaur.

WHO AM I? ART BY RAY BARBER

I am a ghostly ghost.

It's your friend, Noodles.

I am not a mouse
crawling into a bag.

I am a jolly fisherman.

Leave it to Noodles
to capture the puzzle idea
in "Cheep, Cheep, I am not a Sheep,"
and put himself
right in the middle of it!
Perhaps the children
would like to follow Noodles' lead
and create their own
upside-down puzzles.

20

I am not a snail
creeping along.

I am an astronaut.

I am a fat hen
sitting on my eggs.

I am not an ice cream cone.

If your children are not acquainted with the friendly ghost Noodles, you may wish to borrow a copy of *Sounds I Remember*, where Noodles first appears. One thing is certain. The children and Noodles will be fast friends before long.

I am not a sea horse
swimming around.

I am a frightened little kid.

I am not a flame
blowing in the wind.

I'm Not a Hot Dog!

I'm a hound dog.

A STORY BY BILL MARTIN JR.
PICTURES BY DAVID GANTZ

A hot dog can't run.
I can.

24

A hot dog can't play.

I can.

baby
hungry

sparrow
worm

won't
doesn't

fly.
growl.

A hot dog can't work.
I can.

For a discussion of this important linguistic technique that is developed throughout *Sounds of Language,* see T E page 75.

A hot dog can't sing.
I can.

Have the children fallen in love with this personable basset
hound? If so, they may wish to tell or write their own stories
about him. Or would they rather tell and write about their own
or their friend's dog?

A hot dog can't sleep with you.
I can—

until your mother comes in.

When an author gets a repetitive pattern going, he has
to find some way to break the pattern or the story
will never end. How do the children like this author's
ending?

THE LETTERMEN

drawing by Tom Huffman

These pages suggest a letter hunt.
Can the children find
their initials?
The letters
in their first names?
The whole alphabet?
Would they like to create
their own lettermen?

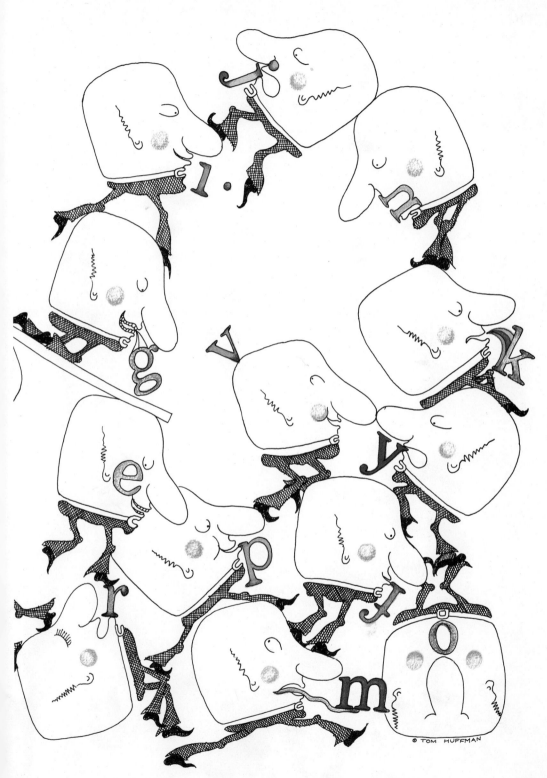

© TOM HUFFMAN

35

Chocolate goo.

five

unlocking
considerations
without causing
them to loose their
toe-hold on either
the sentence or
the story.

It is critical in helping children develop
linguistic power that we never leave
a word or story in a fractured
shape. We should always
bring the skillbuilding
full circle—back to the
ineffable dance of syl-
lables in which senten-
ces and meanings have
their being.

Pudding mix.

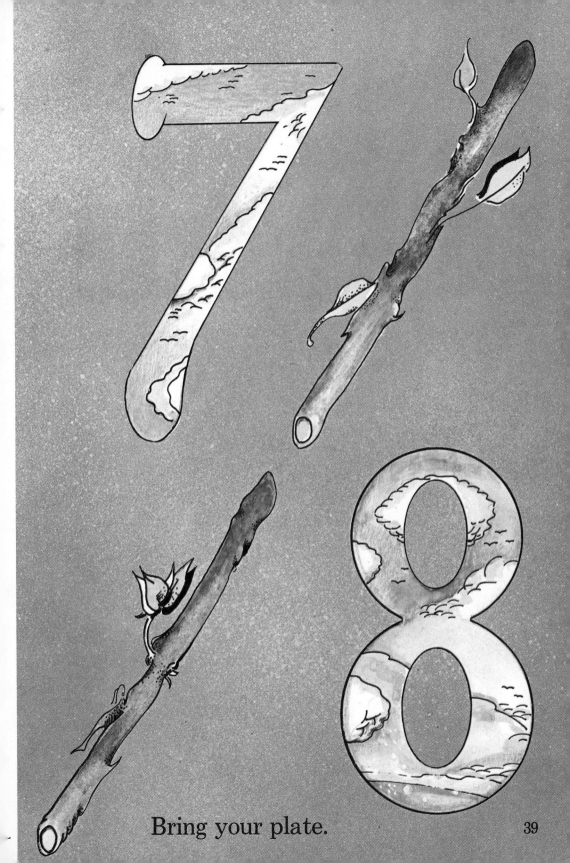

Bring your plate.

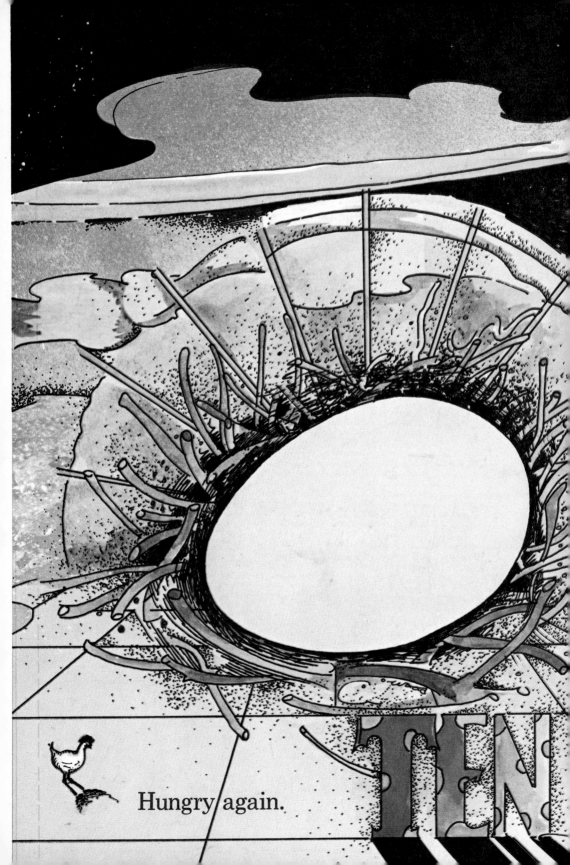

Hungry again.

TEN

Who Did? Who Did?

AN OLD RHYME, ART BY RAY BARBER

Boys: Who did?

Girls: Who did?

Boys: Who did?

Girls: Who did?

All: **Who did swallow Jo-Jo-Jo?**

This old rhyme can be chanted with no thought of meaning. Children will easily take it in through the ear and can then be helped to analyze the printed form of the language. They will notice, for example, that when their ears are hearing repetitive patterns, their eyes are seeing repetitions. It is this kind of experience which helps children discover that print works just like talk. This discovery is basic to the development of useful decoding skills.

Boys: Who did?

Girls: Who did?

Boys: Who did?

Girls: Who did?

All: **Who did swallow Jo-Jo-Jo?**

I'm Jonah!

Boys: Who did?

Girls: Who did?

Boys: Who did?

Girls: Who did?

Boys: Who did swallow Jo-nah?

Girls: Who did swallow Jo-nah?

All: **Who did swallow Jo-nah down?**

I'm the whale!

Girls: Whale did.
Boys: Whale did.
Girls: Whale did.
Boys: Whale did.
All: **Whale did swallow Jo-Jo-Jo.**

Girls: Whale did.
Boys: Whale did.
Girls: Whale did.
Boys: Whale did.
All: **Whale did swallow Jo-Jo-Jo.**

Girls: Whale did.
Boys: Whale did.
Girls: Whale did.
Boys: Whale did.
Girls: Whale did swallow Jo-nah.
Boys: Whale did swallow Jo-nah.
All: **Whale did swallow Jo-nah up.**

Boys and Girls:	Gabriel.
Teacher:	Gabriel.
Boys and Girls:	Gabriel.
Teacher:	Gabriel.
All:	**Gabriel blow your trump-trump-trump.**

My new name is Gabriel!

The children will be delighted to know that Noodles is still with them. Best acquaintance with this little ghost who always represents the child's point of view, comes through listening to the cassette recordings that accompany this and other *Sounds of Language* books.

Boys and Girls:	Gabriel.
Teacher:	Gabriel.
Boys and Girls:	Gabriel.
	Gabriel.
	Gabriel blow your trump-trump-trump.

Boys and Girls:	Gabriel.
Teacher:	Gabriel.
Boys and Girls:	Gabriel.
Teacher:	Gabriel.
Boys and Girls:	Gabriel, blow your trum-pet.
Teacher:	Gabriel, blow your trum-pet.
All:	**Gabriel, blow your trum-pet**

loud!

Dressing is Depressing

A JINGLE, ART BY RAY BARBER

Notice how the book becomes a toy as a child turns it around to follow the lettering. This is one way to lessen reading tension. It is also an effective way to heighten a child's curiosity about print and how it works. As the children move their eyes and books to follow the type, they learn in impressive ways that type moves

Button the buttons. Snap the snaps. Hook the hooks. Zip the zippers. Tie the ties. Strap the straps. Clasp the clasps. Slip the slippers. Buckle the buckles. Belt the belts. Brace the braces— Pin the pins. Lace the laces. Loop the loops. Lock the locks. Knot the knots.

What I like best is my own skin—
That's the dress I'm <u>always</u> in.

and that a person must therefore discover where a line of type begins and which way it is going. A dramatic experience like this is more impressive than didactic rules about "begin on the left."

This linguistic picture is an invitation to experiment with an analysis of word endings—*ow* and *own*—as well as with beginning consonants and blends. More importantly, it is a chance for children to experiment with linguistic sequence. They will discover, for example, that the reading can begin with *"Wow, etc.,"* or with *"A brown cow, etc.,"* or with *"How nice! etc."* They also will discover that *how* and *nice* must be kept contingent, just as *A brown cow* must be, otherwise the meanings are destroyed. *Wow Pow* and *Now,* on the other hand, can punctuate the sequence randomly: *Wow, how nice! Pow, Now, a brown cow,* or *A brown cow, Now, how nice! Pow Wow.* And all the while the children are devising new sequences, they are both employing and developing word unlocking skills in a systematic and retrievable manner.

HOW

A BROWN

DESIGN BY ERIC CARLE

Here is a poem that invites children's eyes to see rhyming words while their ears are hearing them. The typographical design invites children to make observations about the pairs of rhyming words: the endings sound alike and look alike; the beginnings sound different and look different. In these kinds of excursions into figuring out how print works, it is important to encourage the children to verbalize their observations in their own words. Don't press for exact answers. As the children feel rewarded by their learnings which occur when they take a good long look at print, they will gradually become habitual analyzers of print and will begin to organize a collection of

There once was a green

Little

Who played in the wood

On a

learnings about written language and how it works. You may wish to help them record these discoveries on a reading chart. This kind of child inquiry into the workings of print with its attendant verbalizing of discoveries, is a qualitatively different experience from having you or a workbook *tell* the children a lot of rules which they then must memorize. There is no such thing as a story or poem which cannot be analyzed for how it works in both its spoken and written form, and SOUNDS OF LANGUAGE takes full advantage of this way for helping children learn to be skilled and joyous decoders of print.

A screech owl sitting

In a  tree! tree! tree!

Came after the frog

With a Scree! Scree! Scree!

When the frog heard the owl

In a **flash! flash! flash!**

This poem will probably create in children the same feelings of intrigue that they have when they encounter a live praying mantis—a time to look and ponder.

The Praying Mantis

Does more than pray,

She helps us in another way.

She eats up many garden lice,

And that, I think, is very nice.

A POEM, AUTHOR UNKNOWN,
PICTURE BY KENNETH DEWEY

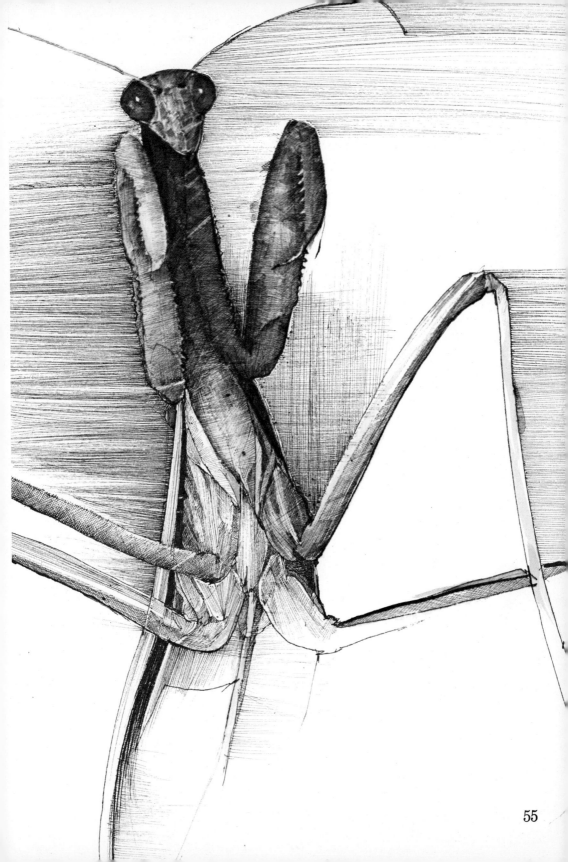

Everybody Says

A SONG BY MALVINA REYNOLDS

Children should hear you read this selection like a joyous, rhythmic chant, and be asked to chime in as they perceive how it goes. No child should be asked to read it alone unless he volunteers or until he has it securely in the ear and on the tongue and can do it "by heart." Word recognitions will inevitably follow in the wake of the chantings.

Everybody says,
"Sit down, sit down."
Everybody says,
"Sit down, sit down."

But I can't sit down,
and I can't sit down,
'Cause my feet are all full
of dance around.

After children know this song and can chime it with linguistic poise and security, invite the children to innovate on the author's pattern. *"Children, supposing we didn't want to use the author's words* sit down. *What else could we have everyone say?"* As the children supply commands such as, *"Don't move," "Keep quiet,"* etc. they will find themselves with a new story to illustrate and put on the reading table. What fun it will be for them to discover how easily they can read their new story, patterned as it is on a familiar structure. For further discussion of ways to develop and use this reading skill, see TE p 19.

Bump deedle ump,

bump bump a dee,

Everybody bump

a deedle dance with me.

Everybody says,
  "Be good, be good."
Everybody says,
  "Be good, be good."

If they understood,
  I'm as good as good,
'Cause dancing around
  is what I should.

Bump deedle ump,
  bump bump a dee,
Everybody bump
  a deedle
  dance with me.

Everybody says,
"What's wrong?
What's wrong?"
Everybody says,
"What's wrong?
What's wrong?"

Well, there's nothing wrong
when I sing my song,
But you'd better look out
if I'm quiet long.

Bump deedle ump,
bump bump a dee,
Everybody bump
a deedle
dance with me.

Shown on the opposite page is the technique of substituting other words for each of the key words in a sentence, thereby using the original structure to express new thoughts. Throughout the program, whenever you and the children come upon a sentence that you like, you may want to write the sentence on the board, and then invite the children to make vocabulary substitutions for the various words. The children can then pick from each column their favorite words and spin a new sentence. For a discussion of this technique, transforming a sentence, see TE page 75.

At Home

This story has many useful sentence patterns that children will find helpful in their personal writing and speaking. As you and the children transform these basic sentences, they can be helped to verbalize the fact that once a person owns a useful sentence pattern,

A STORY BY PATRICIA K. MILLER
AND IRAN L. SELIGMAN,
PICTURES BY JOHN TEPPICH

he also owns hundreds of sentences based on that pattern. Throughout his lifetime he will be encountering transformations of the basic patterns in his speaking and writing and reading.

ON THE ICE

Penguins are birds

but they do not fly.

They swim in the water.

They walk on the ice.

fly	over	roof
run	around	yard
gallop	by	barn

Penguins live
   at the cold South Pole.
They like the snow.
They like the ice.

Millions of penguins,
  living together.
Millions of penguins,
  at home on the ice:

Penguins are birds.
Their feathers keep them
warm and dry.

Penguins eat fish
and grow very fat.
They need their fat
to keep them warm.

Penguins build nests
in the ice and snow.
They line the nests
with little stones.
Here the mother
lays her eggs.

The mother and father
  watch over the nest.
The mother and father
  keep the eggs warm.
They keep the eggs warm
  four or five weeks.
Then the eggs hatch.

73

Penguin chicks are small
and hungry.
The mother and father
feed them fish.
The penguin chicks eat and eat.
Day by day
they grow bigger and fatter.

When they are grown,
  they leave the nest.
They swim in the water
  and dive for fish.

Millions of penguins
  living together.
Millions of penguins
  at home on the ice.

Three Little Bugs

in a basket,
Hardly room for two;
One looks like her, one looks like him
And one looks just like you.

AN OLD JINGLE, ART BY RAY BARBER

After the children have enjoyed their own ways for bouncing a ball with this rhyme, they may wish to try these traditional ball-bouncing routines.

A Bounce-the-Ball Rhyme

AN OLD JINGLE

Jack, Jack, pump the water;
(Bounce the ball normally.)
Jack, Jack, pump the water;

Jack, Jack, pump the water;

Pump the water, Jack.

Jack, Jack, jump the water;
(Lift one leg over the bouncing ball.)
Jack, Jack, jump the water;

Jack, Jack, jump the water;

Jump the water, Jack.

Jack, Jack, go under the water;
(Bounce the ball under the leg.)
Jack, Jack, go under the water;

Jack, Jack, go under the water;

Go under the water, Jack.

Boys,
your

is not allowed
not

POW

80

LOUD
LOUDer
LOUDest noise

This design in sound incorporates the comparative forms of an adjective, together with some language tom-foolery. If you're in sound mental and physical form, you might enjoy having the children let themselves go on *loud, louder, loudest,* with a special Fourth-of-July explosion on *POW-WOW.* This may not endear you to your principal, but it certainly will cement the word recognitions in kids' heads.

a LOUD
WOW

Witch,
Witch,
which one of us
are you looking for?
If it's I
you spy,
look no more.
I just escaped
through a crack
In the floor.

This is one of those "take-over" language experiences which children will claim as their own on one or two hearings. After the language is in their "blood and bones," keep it active by giving fresh suggestions about its interpretation from day to day. For example, one day you might suggest that the children read it like a spooky story, the next day like a television commercial, the next day like a Halloween song, etc., etc. Keeping the familiar active with new motivation is a basic teaching technique that releases both you and children to creativeness simultaneously with cementing the learnings.

A JINGLE BY BILL MARTIN JR.
DRAWING BY SHELLEY FRESHMAN

83

As you encounter innovative arrangements of type in this book, you may be surprised at how confidently your children are willing to attack such pages. We adults have grown accustomed to school books where the same size and style of type move relentlessly from left to right, page after page, and it is easy to forget that today's children are encountering imaginative and flamboyant uses of type on T.V., in magazine advertising and even on their cereal boxes. How appropriate that school books too can call upon imaginative and intriguing page design in an effort to bring new dimensions to the children's linguistic learnings and to convince today's young readers that there is much that is alive and gripping between the covers of a book.

Backward day?
So let it be:

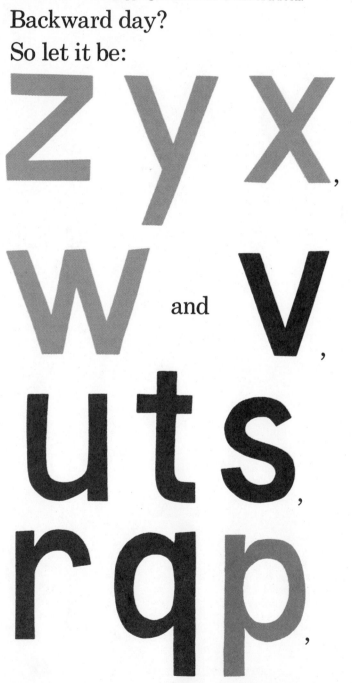

z y x,

w and v,

u t s,

r q p,

o n m,
l k j,
and   k   and a big long
i h g,
f e d,

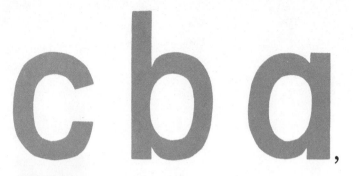

c b a,

the backward way.

BACKWARD DAY

BY NOODLES

LETTERS BY ERIC CARLE

Boom! Boom! Boom!

on the big bass drum,
This is the way to do it,
Get a drum stick for a well-trained dog
And let the dog go to it.

A JINGLE, ART BY LEON WINIK

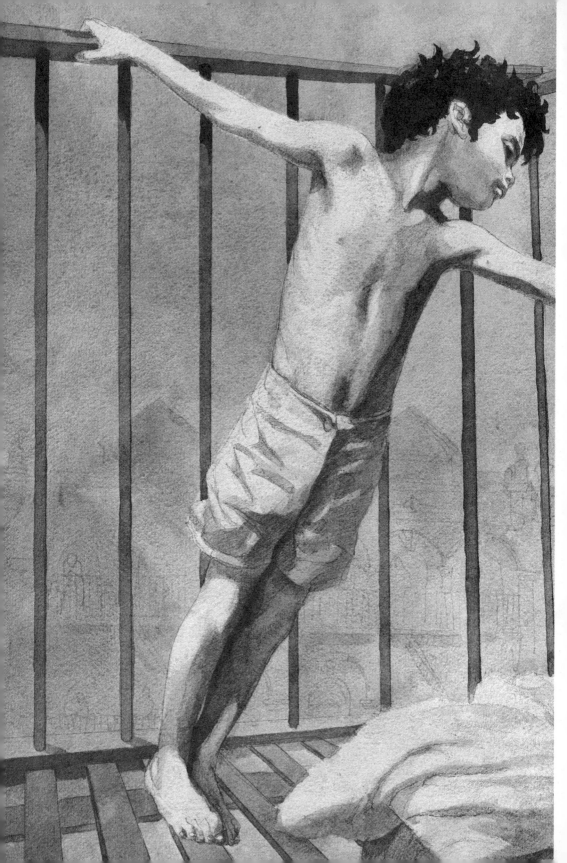

Bird in the Building-Tree

BY BILL MARTIN JR. WITH PAINTINGS BY SYMEON SHIMIN

Here is a day
in the life of a city
child. Read the story as
a literary and art
experience, without
attempting in any way
to develop the concepts
involved. As the
children move in and
out of the pages, notions
like "bird in the building
tree" will move in and
out of their awareness,
satisfying their human
yen for being lifted out
of ordinary ways for
saying things.

At eight o'clock

in the morning,

Bird in the building-tree,

After the children have enjoyed the story several times, it might be interesting to let the children read the pictures, supplying their own language. Won't it be interesting to hear their interpretations of who this boy is, where he is, and what he is doing?

At nine o'clock in the morning,

Singing merrily,

Watch the children as
you read the story
aloud. When did it
occur to them that the
story is hung together
by intervals of time?

At ten o'clock

He ventures out,

At eleven o'clock

He hops about,

Did this youngster
make his own sandwich
or was it left for him
by some member of the family
who perhaps is gone for the day?
There are no "right" answers
to such a question.
The responses are valuable
because they give us insight
into children's experiences
and language ways.

At twelve o'clock

He flies alone,

Back to the building-tree.

At one o'clock in the afternoon,
Reaching quietly,

The rhythm of the story and particularly of these lines make the word *curiously* a natural and easy encounter. Even if children have not heard it before, they will sense its meaning and syllabic structure, and ever after read it like an "old friend." This is a qualitatively different vocabulary experience from dealing with the word *curiously* in a word list.

At two o'clock in the afternoon,

Watching curiously,

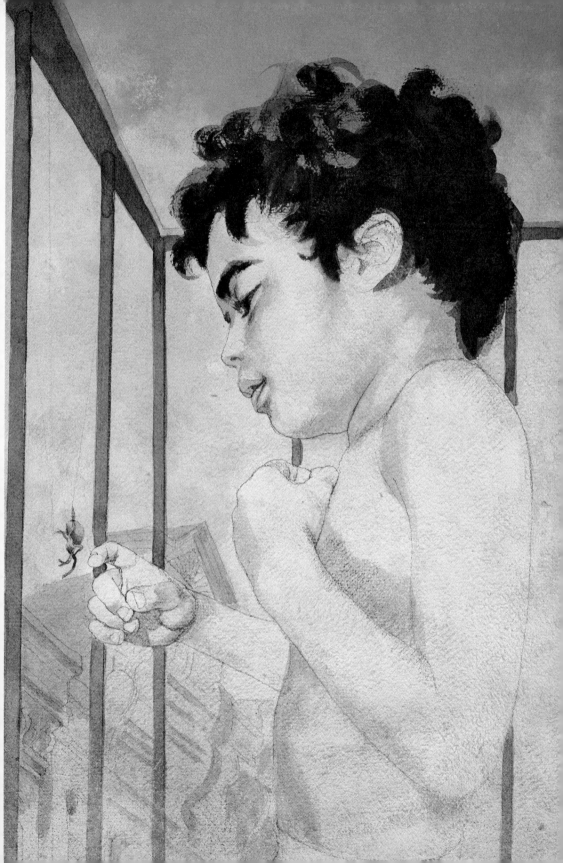

At three o'clock,

A summer rain,

At four o'clock,

The sun again,

The children's spontaneous responses will probably clue you in on where to go next. Would they like to hear the story again? Would they like to read along with you? Would they like to talk about their own important morning-'til-night time intervals? Would they like to talk about this child who seems to own the fire escape on his building? Whatever you do, don't ask those tight little comprehension questions which demand right and wrong answers. You and the children and the story all deserve something better.

At five o'clock the bird is back,

Safe in the building-tree.

THE LETTERMEN

Looking at vowels

drawing by Tom Huffman

Sound the missing
vowels, kids, good
and loud:
H-pp- b-rthd-y t- y--!
H-pp- b-rthd-y t- y--!
H-pp- b-rthd-y d--r
N-dl-s,
H-pp- b-rthd-y
t- y--!

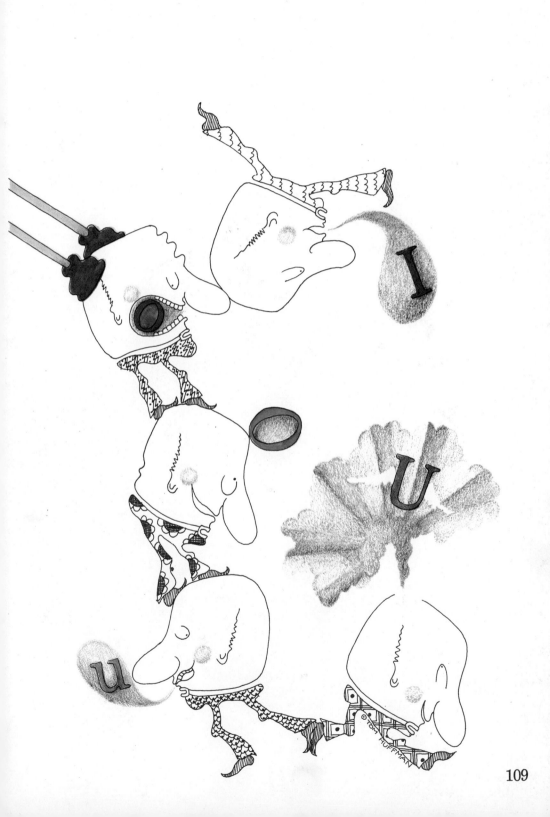

A Story by Noodles

ILLUSTRATIONS BY DAVID GANTZ

If the children listen to the Bill Martin cassette recordings, they will soon discover that Noodles has a
cat. What better model can this little ghost set for
the children than to write a story about his pet?

This is my cat.

She never eats at small table

He always sleeps on the big chair
in the living room.

kitchen.

113

Here is one of the most
frequently used sentence patterns
in the English language.
Would the children like to transform it
so they can see how easily
a basic sentence can become
dozens of new sentences
for their speaking and writing?
See T E page 75.

When I

come home

from school,

he

wakes

up.

Don't be surprised if the children want to imitate Noodles when they read his story. This little ghost who represents a child's point of view, is recognized by the children as a real friend.

When you pick him up in the middle,
he droops at both ends.

When he's full,

he turns on his motor and purrs.

When words look like they sound, children are helped to discover that print works like talk.

Sometimes the kids dress him up
and push him in a buggy.

He doesn't like that.

Do you blame him?

Sometimes he just sits
in a tree and thinks.

About what?

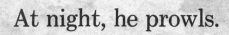

At night, he prowls.

In the morning, he's always
at the back door waiting for me.

"Children,
do you suppose
we could write another chapter
in the life of Noodles and his cat?
Supposing we started our story *One day* . . ."

I am a Gold Lock

AN OLD RHYME, ART BY RAY BARBER

Me: I am a gold lock.

You: I am a gold key.

Me: I am a silver lock.

You: I am a silver key.

Me: I am a brass lock.

You: I am a brass key.

Me: I am a lead lock.

You: I am a lead key.

Me: I am a monk lock.

      I am a monk key.

As Tommy Snooks and Bessy Brooks
were walking out on Monday,
Said Tommy Snooks to Bessy Brooks,
"Yesterday was Sunday."

A MOTHER GOOSE RHYME,
DRAWINGS BY PAPAS

As the children decipher Noodles' Halloween sounds, they will have an intriguing way for appreciating the fact that letters do represent sounds. For example, will they choose to pronounce the oooo's as long $\bar{o}$ or as $\overline{oo}$. Either pronunciation is acceptable. It is the children's discussion leading to their choices that matters.

OOOO

'Tis the night of Halloween

ooooooo eeeeeee O

Children might like to experiment with other Halloween sounds, created with letters and combinations of letters. A bulletin board full of wheee's and oodeley-oodeley's will do more good than a whole semester of pale purple ditto sheets on phonics.

OOOO

ZZZZZZZZZ

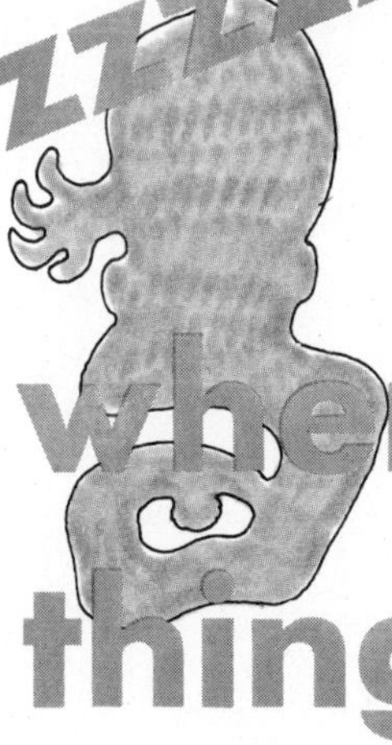

when ghostly things are seen.

OOOOO

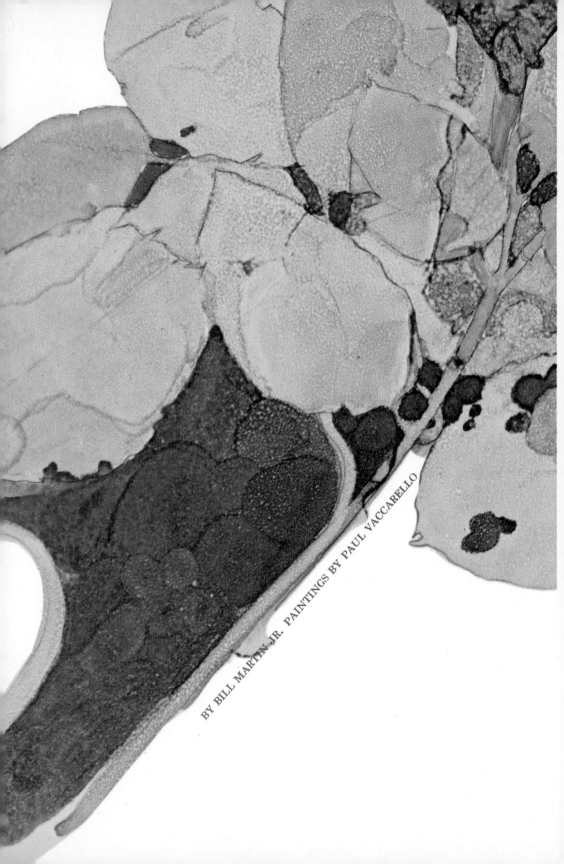

BY BILL MARTIN JR. PAINTINGS BY PAUL VACCARELLO

The first little caterpillar
crawled into a bower.

This story is hung together around a familiar cultural sequence, ordinal number, and a rhyme scheme. As you are reading aloud, notice how the children latch on to the basic patterns (and the vocabulary) in the story, even though they don't verbalize what they have discovered. For a discussion of the use of literary structure in decoding print, see TE p. 38.

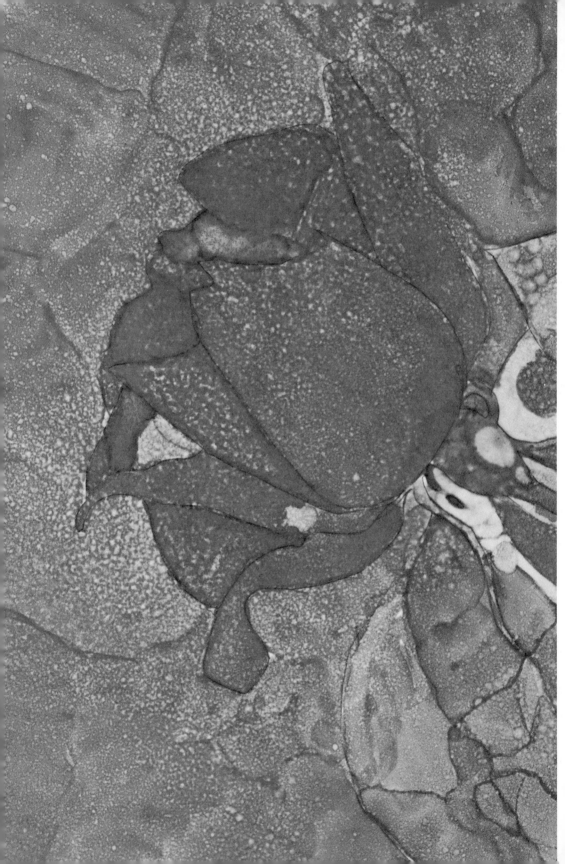

After hearing you read this story aloud several times, children will begin to chime in, and finally will be reading it on their own without ever realizing that they've been having a reading lesson. Don't hurry them. Just read and enjoy the story for no other purpose, and the children's skills will develop naturally.

The second little caterpillar wriggled up a flower.

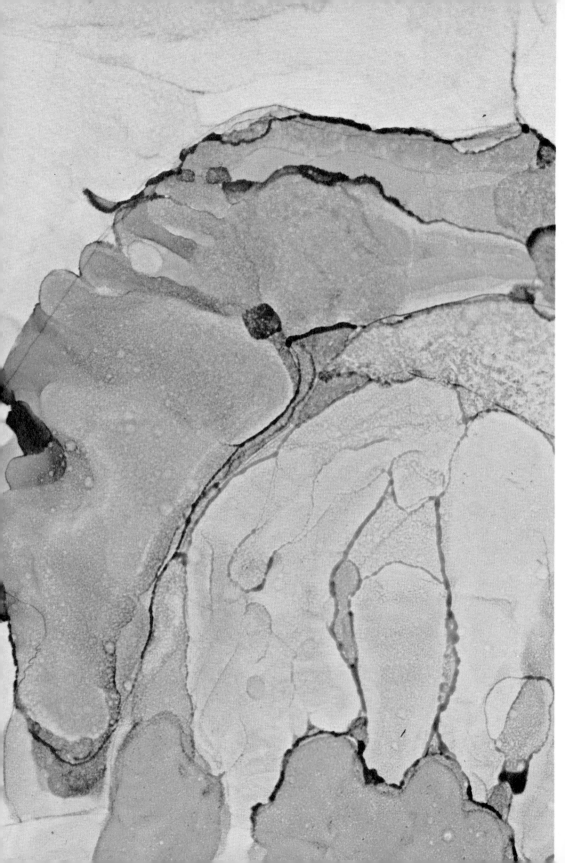

The third little caterpillar
climbed a cabbage head.

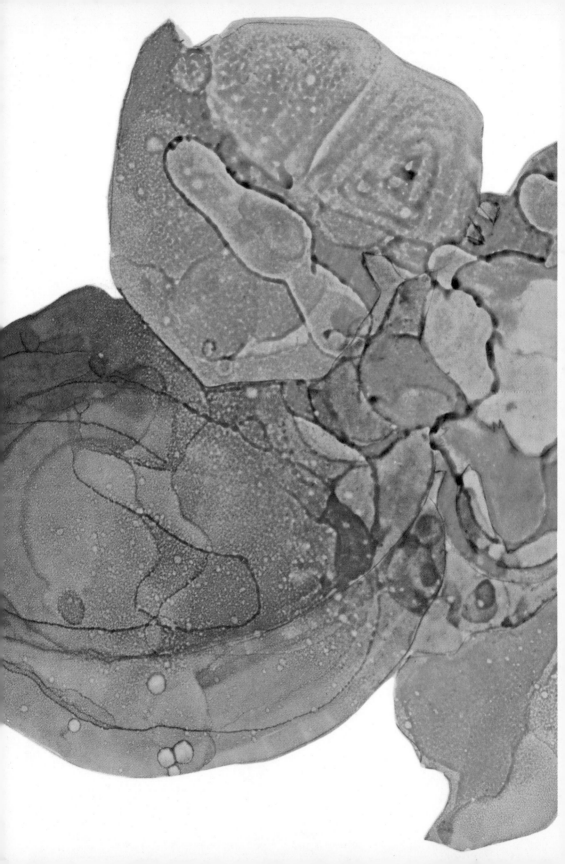

The fourth little caterpillar found a melon bed.

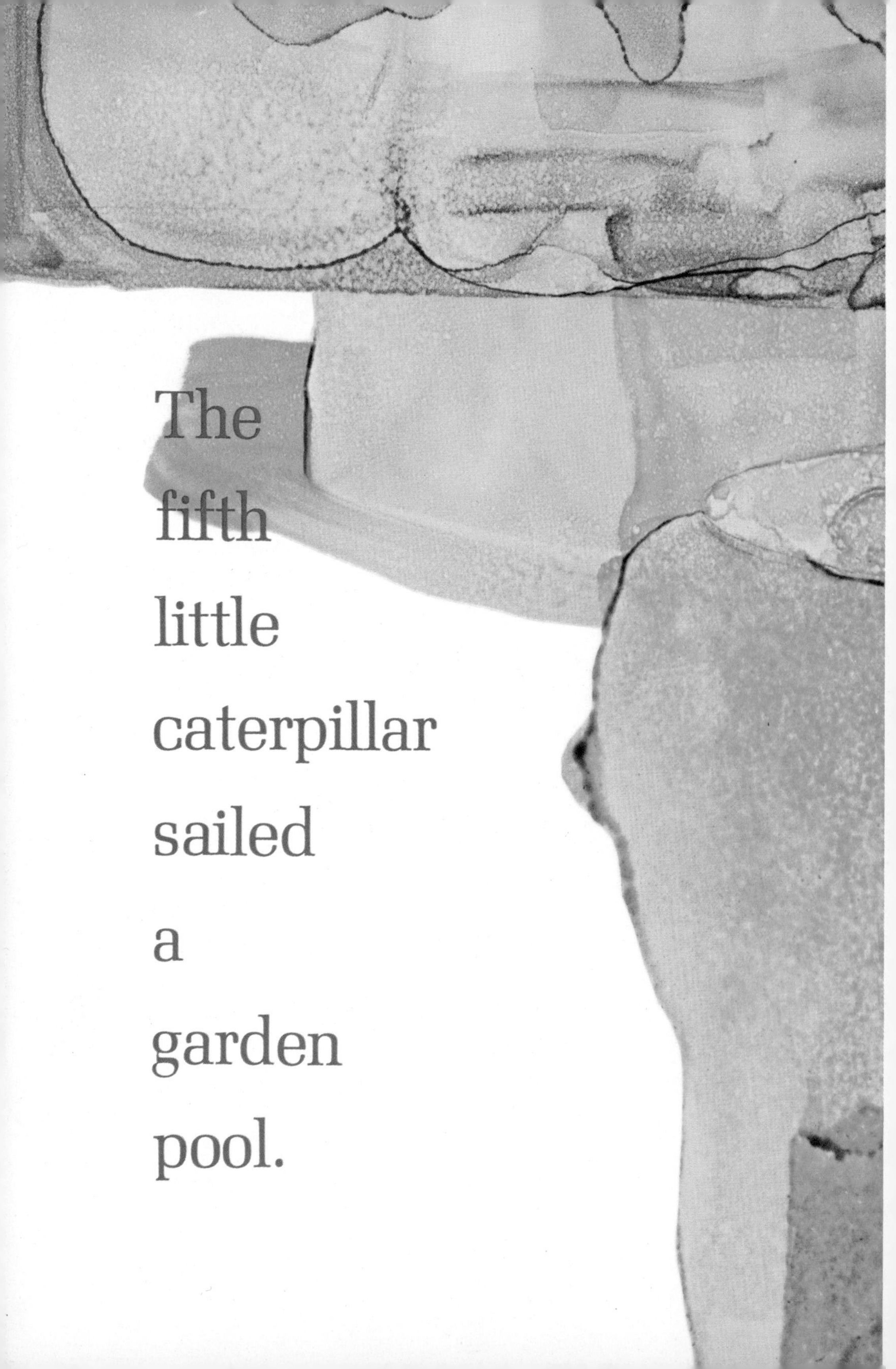

The

fifth

little

caterpillar

sailed

a

garden

pool.

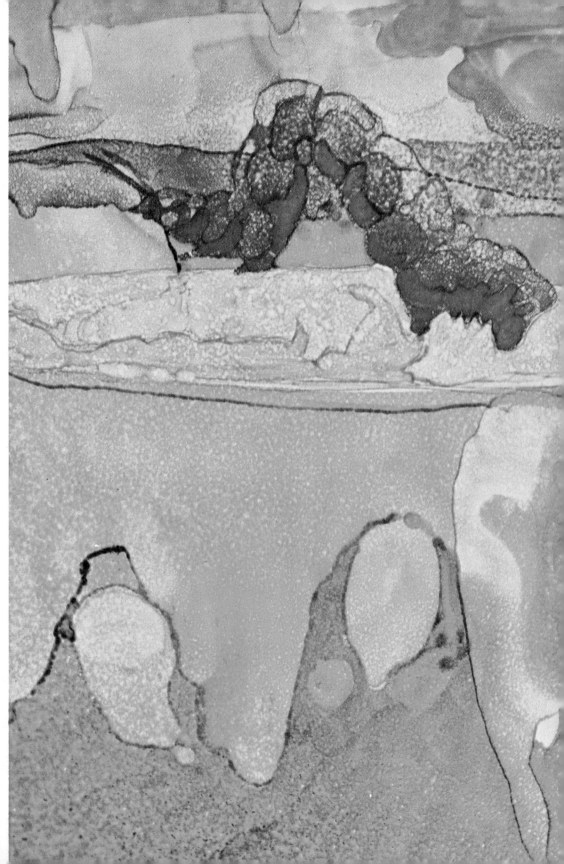

The

sixth

little

caterpillar

was

carried

off

to

school.

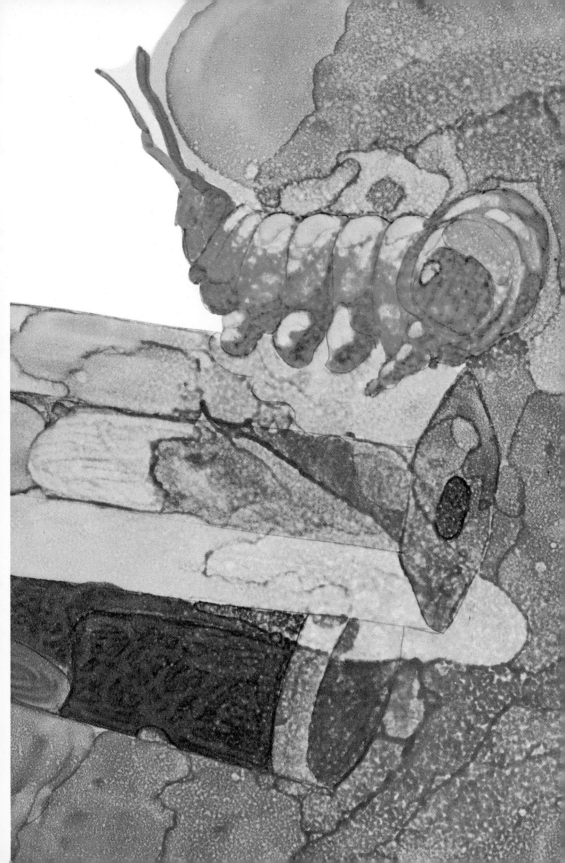

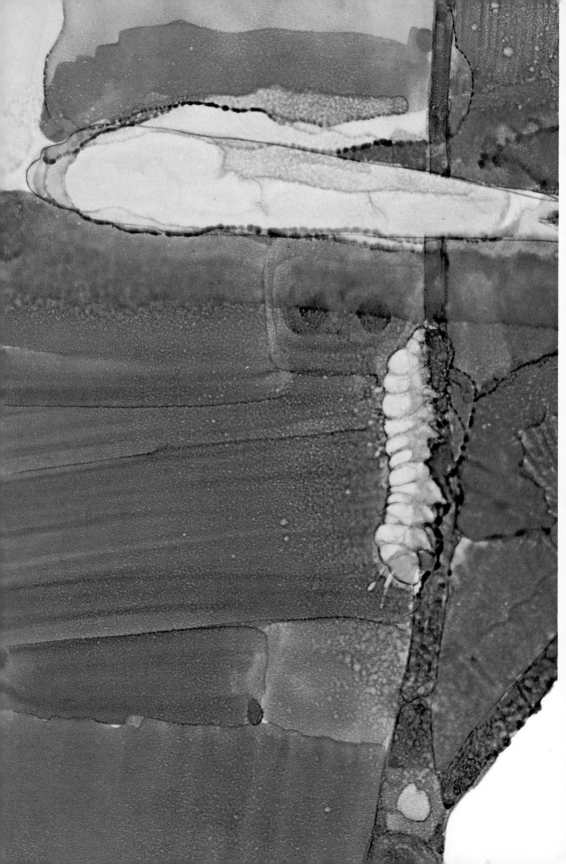

The seventh little caterpillar
met a hungry wren.

Observe how this shift of page
design adds a pleasurable
respite from the traditional.
We turned this illustration to
give the bird's tail more
"breathing" space, but the
psychological effect is an
intrigue that gives the reader a
sudden sense of aliveness.

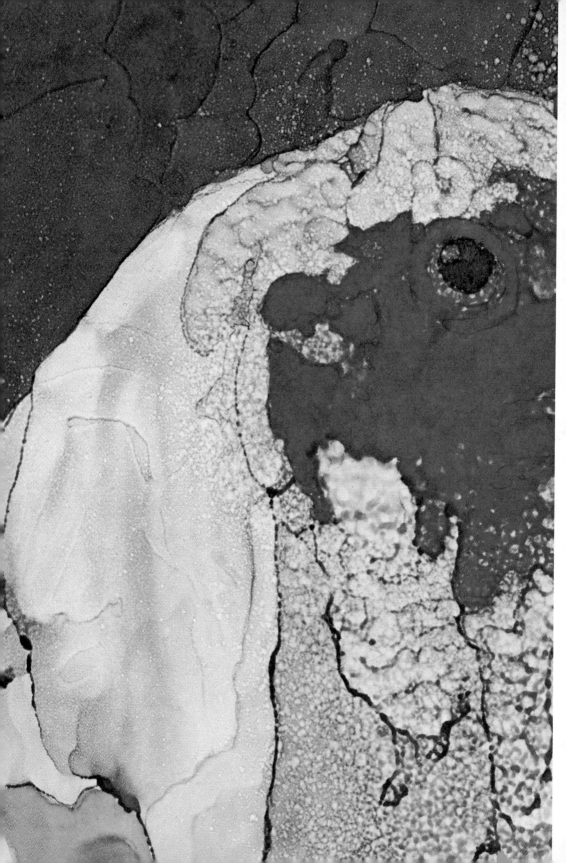

The eighth little caterpillar
was frightened by a hen.

The ninth little caterpillar
fell into the sea.

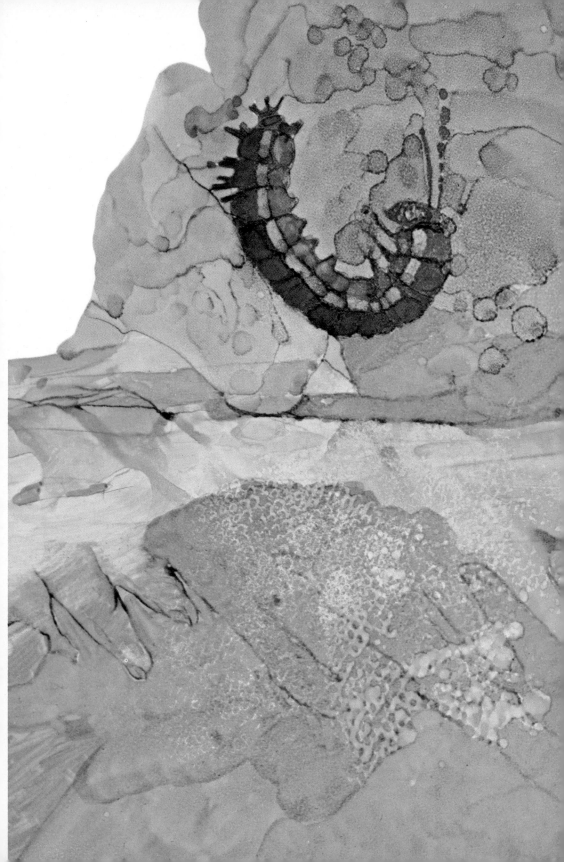

The tenth little caterpillar
scaled an apple tree,

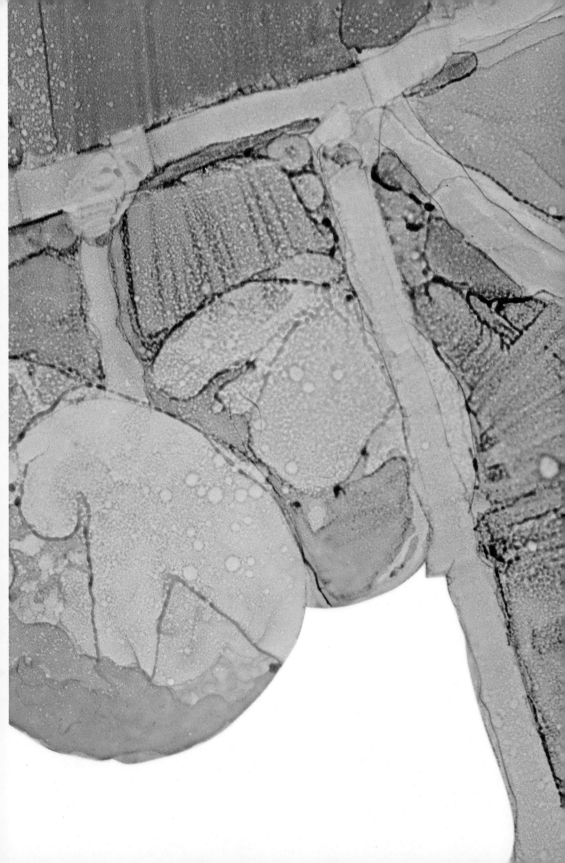

And hung there patiently,

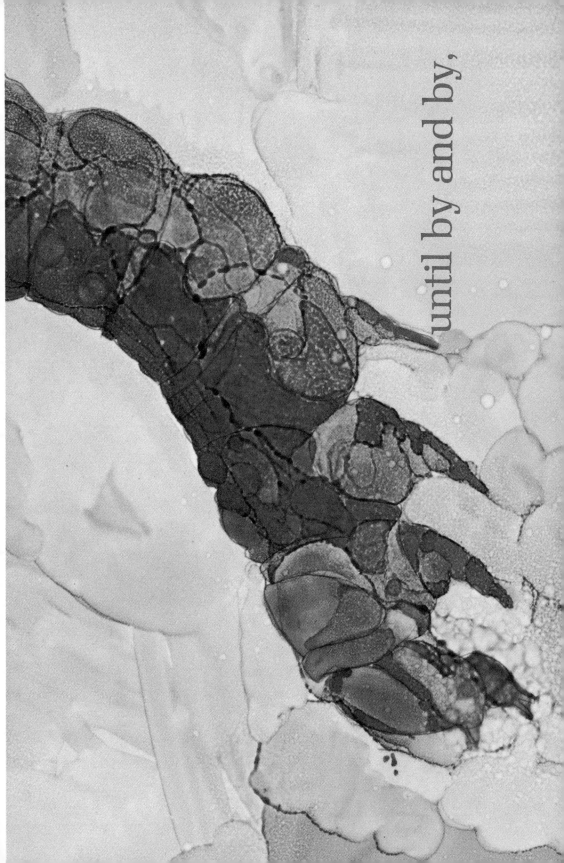

until by and by,

the

tenth

little

caterpillar

became

a

butterfly.

I Feel Pretty,

oh, so pretty,
I feel pretty and witty and bright!
And I pity
any girl who isn't me
tonight.

I feel charming,
oh, so charming,
It's alarming how charming I feel!
And so pretty
that I hardly can believe
I'm real.

A SONG BY STEPHEN SONDHEIM
WITH MUSIC BY LEONARD BERNSTEIN,
PAINTING BY MURIEL WOOD

157

My Brother was a Fisherman

He fished in the sea,

And all the fish that he could catch

Were one, two, three.

AN OLD RHYME,
PICTURE BY KELLY OECHSLI

My brother brought the fishes home,

He brought them from the shore.

When seven sat to savor them,

He wished he'd caught some more.

Let the children figure out from the shape of the sentence that
the word *savor* tells that those 7 people are doing something to
the fish. After exploring all of their hunches, what fun for them
to discover that what those people are doing is
sitting at the table getting great pleasure from
"smelling and tasting" the fish.

159

You'd better run, hound dog!

So long! It's been good to know you!

So long! It's been good to know you!

It surely has!!!

Part One

The Heart of the Program

The *Sounds of Language* reading program
is a fresh and enchanting collection
of poems, stories, articles, and pictures
that realistically prompt children to hear the spoken patterns
of the sentences they read.
As children gain skill in using their ears
to guide their eyes in reading,
they have a qualitatively different reading experience.

little Indians, 4 little, 3 little, 2 little Indians, 1 little Indian boy. 1 little, 2 little, 3 little Indians, 4 little, 5 little, 6 little

Consider the young child
who has frequently heard his teacher read
"Ten Little Indians."
Once a child has these sounds
clearly and solidly in his ear,
he has little difficulty reading this old rhyme
in its printed form.
Once his ears begin telling him
what his eyes are seeing,
he approaches the reading with confidence and expectation.
And when he comes to his teacher and exultingly declares,

I know that word, Miss Barber!
That word is "little!"

she has evidence
that he is relating sight and sound in reading.
And it is easy for her to take this child a step further
by asking him if he can find the number 4,
or if he can find the word *Indian.*
It should not surprise you to know
that even at the first-grade level,
a child is already something of an expert
in analyzing language,
a fact overlooked in most reading programs.

Think of the three-year-old child on a bus
who says,

> I rang the bell.

a sentence sound he learned by listening.
At age four, he is apt to say,

> I ringed the bell.

a sentence sound that he never in his life heard.
Why then does he say it?
A child at four no longer simply imitates language sounds
that he hears in his environment.
He is beginning to figure out how language works
and how to make it work for him.
When he says, *I ringed the bell,*
he gives evidence that he is analyzing language
and that he knows how to change a verb
from present to past tense.

In similar ways in the *Sounds of Language* program,
a child is helped to become more and more expert in
using and analyzing language.
The aim is to help him become aware
of what he intuitively knows about language,
and to help him explore and verbalize
old and new learnings.

—from *Sounds I Remember*

5 little, 6 little, 7 little Indians, 8 little, 9 little, 10 little Indian boys. 10 little Indians, 9 little, 8 little, 7 little, Indians,

Language analysis emerges in abundance
at all levels in *Sounds of Language*
because the program is a total language and esthetic experience
which logically and comfortably connects a child
with his past experiences in using oral language
and with his intuitive knowledge of how language works.

Too many children in school have come to know reading
as word calling and drill,
with little or no opportunity
to claim language in its many dimensions.
The purposes of this teacher's edition, therefore,
are to help you join children and support them

1) in their growing appreciation of literature and language;

2) in a useful inquiry into how language works,
       both in its oral and written traditions;

3) in a useful inquiry into literary structure; and

4) in the development of esthetic awareness.

The pages of the pupil book (incorporated in this teacher's edition)
have been annotated for your convenience.
The annotations appear at the precise spot on the page
where they are needed to point up learning insights
and teaching strategies.

At no time is an annotation so prescriptive
that it precludes your insights from the teaching process.
To the contrary, the annotations are geared
to triggering all your insights and hunches
in helping children *latch on* to language and their humanity.

There is nothing complicated about this method of teaching.
Once you have read this informal dialogue
and the annotated pages,
you will feel comfortably at home with the program.
In fact, you may find yourself thinking:
Here, at last, is a program that helps me
use all of my knowledge and intuitions about language
—and about teaching.

Now, let's talk informally
about ways for using the *Sounds of Language* readers
to bring new dimensions
into your teaching of reading.
We have no choice but to help
all children learn to read.
They inherit the need to read
simply by living in our culture.
We, therefore, have the obligation to provide
wide-ranging ways for unlocking print.

What works for one child
doesn't necessarily work for another child.
What works for one kind of reading material
doesn't necessarily work for another.
Children are highly inventive and insightful
in ways of unlocking print—
until unimaginative reading instruction
tells them there is only one way to decode,
"Sound out the words!"
Actually, there are dozens of ways
to unlock the printed page.
And there are dozens of ways
that lead into the act of learning to read
before successfully pulling together
ear and eye and tongue and muscle
in the mature act of reading.

Some boys we have known
seemed at first to read more with their feet
than they did with their eyes.
You've had these kinds of boys
in your own classrooms.

Aren't they interesting
as they screw themselves up
into impossible positions
and keep perfect time to whatever is being read?
We should be saying to these boys:

> *Henry, you're so great at reading
> with your feet! How would you
> like to try reading with your eyes?*

And Henry wouldn't mind at all—
in fact he might be delighted to try—
knowing his comfortable way for responding to print
has been so respected.
But unfortunately,
we don't recognize Henry's rhythmical body response
as a reading behavior,
accustomed as we are to thinking about reading
as an eye exercise
and a "sounding-out" ritual.
Instead of praising Henry
and helping him include other parts of his body
in his response to the printed page,
we are likely to admonish:

> *Now, Henry, sit up straight
> and pay attention to your book.*

If Henry had the skill of self-analysis
and dared challenge the teacher's edict,
he might respond:

> *But I am paying attention.*
> *Rhythmical body response*
> *is part of reading a book.*

Only Henry doesn't have the language
for verbalizing his intuitive response to print.
And unless we have the awareness
to recognize what he is doing,
another potentially successful reader
will start the long and uncomfortable journey
of finding out that there is something wrong
with his way for learning to read;
and another potentially fine teacher
will be thrown into miscommunication with a child
simply because the definition of reading behavior
which has been made available to her
through teachers guides and college courses
is too narrow to accept and encourage
the many-faceted reading behaviors of real live children.

The *Sounds of Language* program makes it easy and enjoyable
for children and teachers to explore and perfect
multiple ways for unlocking print
and enjoying the miracle of language.
Children will learn to figure out the pattern
back of an author's way of putting a story
or poem or sentence together,
and to use this information for reading words
they didn't know they knew.
They will learn to figure out the different shapes of sentences
and to recognize unknown words
largely by where they fall in a sentence.
They will learn to figure out rhyme schemes and read new words
by recognizing where they fall in a certain rhyming slot.
They will learn to figure out underlying rhythmical patterns
and to use syllabic patterns
as one way to take hold of unknown words.

All of this, at first, may sound strange and complex
if you have not observed children using these natural ways
for making a go of reading.
But this essay will help you discover a multiplicity of ways
for using literature to bring new dimensions
into the teaching of reading.
The program is based on only a few practical teaching strategies.
These strategies work in kindergarten
as well as they work in eighth grade and all up and down the line.
The children themselves modify the strategies
by their individualized responses.

Once you own these strategies,
you can forget about the teacher's guide
and look forward to relaxed and creative reading sessions
where you are free to respond
to the children's individualized responses
and where you have a structural know-how
to help them learn to read.

The teaching strategies
explored in this essay are:

1) Recognizing That Language Works in Chunks of Meaning

2) Reading Aloud to Deposit Literary and Linguistic Structures
   in Children's Storehouses

3) Innovating on Literary Structure to Claim Basic Patterns

4) Figuring Out How Stories and Poems Work

5) Helping Children Verbalize Their Intuitive Literary Insights

6) Figuring Out How Sentences Work

7) Innovating on Sentence Patterns

8) Figuring Out How Words Work

9) Figuring Out How Print Works

10) Developing Skill in Comprehension

11) Linking Writing to Reading

12) Cultivating Literary and Esthetic Appreciation

13) Developing Sensitivity to the Three Levels of Language

14) Developing Sensitivity to Humanness

—drawings from "My Mother is the Most Beautiful Woman in the World,"
Sounds of a Young Hunter

Learning to read
is not something that happens
after a stereotyped readiness period
in first grade or kindergarten.
Learning to read
is the job of a lifetime.
Two-and-three-year-old children who are read to a lot
begin their reading careers early.
The day a child gets hold of a sentence pattern that works for him
and reads it into the telephone directory
or the Montgomery Ward catalog
or his daddy's newspaper at night,
he is launching himself on his reading career.
He is role-playing himself as a successful reader.
The day a child reads a book from memory,
he is furthering his reading career.

He, in truth, is finding joy and power
in the pages of a book,
a psychological posture that every successful reader
continuously brings to each reading encounter,
knowing, subconsciously if not consciously,
that he can make a go of print.
This is the first and foremost reading skill.

Part Two

The Teaching Strategies for Sounds of Language

Whether it be at home or at school,
when children are read to,
they begin their naturalistic ways
for latching on to print
and they continue to expand and refine these ways
throughout the course of a lifetime—
provided they are given helpful opportunities.
The *Sounds of Language* teaching strategies
will help you provide these opportunities
for children to respond to print
in naturalistic intuitive ways;
and they also will help you release children
to verbalizing their intuitive responses to language and print,
and develop them into word-unlocking skills.

1 RECOGNIZING THAT LANGUAGE WORKS IN CHUNKS OF MEANING

As each of us learned to speak the language,
simply by imitating the speech sounds that we heard,
we learned to cluster words into meaningful units within a sentence.
Even as babies using nonsense syllables,
we used intonation and clustering
to create a *sound of sense.*
Later as we learned vocabulary and sentence ways,
we made full use of sentence sounds (sometimes called melodies)
demonstrating that we intuitively understood
that language works in chunks of meaning.
Not once did we isolate the word sounds
from the sentence sound in which they were cast.
Not one of us said,

> "*I* (pause) *want* (pause) *my* (pause) *mommy!*".

Rather "*Iwanmymommy!*"
came out as a meaningful linguistic whole,
a fluid sentence sound with a cultural melody
that conveyed both feeling and thought.
Unfortunately, language instruction in schools
has ignored the natural workings of language
by such unnatural techniques as

A) focusing word recognition skills on individual words
rather than on the clustering of words within a sentence,

B) insisting on paragraph forms
with rigid right-left hand margins that ignore
the natural grouping of words within a sentence,

C) talking about word meaning as if a word
actually has a meaning outside the context of the
sentence in which it derived its meaning; and,

D) insisting that children in all of their school language activities
perpetuate these misconceptions.

The poets, more than anyone else in our society,
have tended to improve
the communication potential of their writing
by arranging their words into natural linguistic clusterings.

All of us are familiar with the ragged right hand margin of a poem
and may never have stopped to think
why the sentences are written this way.
Just observe how Margaret Wise Brown
accommodates the lines in "Four Fur Feet"
to the chunks of meaning within each sentence:

OH, he walked along the river

on his four fur feet,

his four fur feet,

his four fur feet.

He walked along the river

on his four fur feet

and heard the boats go toot—O.

—Sounds of a Powwow

Recognizing That Language Works in Chunks of Meaning TE 13

How different this is from a page of prose in an ordinary book
where each line must move rigidly
from a left hand margin to a right hand margin
with only the paragraph breaks
to give a feeling of structure to the printed language.
This inflexible technique cruelly severs words in half
in order to accommodate the margins,
as well as ignoring the natural clustering of words
into chunks of meaning within each sentence.
Let's see what a prose sentence would look like
if it were separated into its chunks of meaning
to enhance the linguistic design of the sentence
rather than the arbitrary width of the page.

> *I looked up*
>
> *with the water running off my face*
>
> *and saw a butterfly,*
>
> *bouncing from blossom to blossom*
>
> *like butterflies do.*
>
> —"Oh, Lord, I Wish I Was a Buzzard," *Sounds in the Wind*

As you observed, this is a complex sentence to read
but how much easier it becomes
when it is printed in its chunks of meaning.
Each of these groups of words has a meaning
that is more important than any single word within the group.
The words in each group, therefore, must be read together
as a subset of the more important set, the sentence.
Each subset leads into the next,
gradually amalgamating into the whole meaning of the sentence.
One of the miracles of our language
is its way of working in chunks of meaning.

An experienced reader does not move through a sentence
by reading each word separately.
Even though language is not ordinarily printed in chunks of meaning,
he learns to see—and sense—the groups of words
that best create meaning.
When a sentence is written from margin to margin across a column or
a page, with no special emphasis on the chunks of meaning, the reader
must do the work of seeing the words in clusters that release meaning.

This, at first, is not an easy task, but it is rewarding
because, soon, the reader finds himself
able to manage material that ordinarily would have stopped him.
Consider the problem of an inexperienced reader
who breaks a sentence into malfunctioning units, like this:

1) *Ayee, Mother do*

2) *not leave*

3) *us, for*

4) *we have*

5) *formed a chain and you*

6) *are the clasp that binds us.*

—"The Grandmother," *Sounds Jubilee*

Such a child has a comprehension problem immediately
because he has violated the linguistic units within the sentence.
Just try reading the sentence orally as it is grouped here
and you will shudder at the absence of the sound of sense.
*The only criterion for knowing a chunk of meaning when you see it
is to hear it.*
A child's intuition about language,
once he has developed the concept of chunks of meaning,
will lead him through the sentence this way,
simply because this is the way he would speak it
and thereby exploit its sound of sense:

1) *Ayee, Mother, do not leave us,*

2) *for we have formed a chain*

3) *and you are the clasp that binds us.*

Reading instruction that emphasizes single word recognition
above all else
actually creates reading problems for children
because units of meaning are torn rudely apart
and children are not freed
to use their accumulated linguistic insights.
The concept of chunks of meaning within a sentence
is not foreign to children,
because they naturally speak in chunks of meaning
as they frame their oral sentences.
They need only to be helped to see that they can recreate
these same chunks on the printed page,
even if books are not printed in this way.
Hopefully the day will come when books,
at least for elementary school children,
will have considerable material printed in spoken language patterns.

2 READING ALOUD TO DEPOSIT LITERARY AND LINGUISTIC STRUCTURES IN CHILDREN'S STOREHOUSES

Each of us has a linguistic storehouse
into which we deposit patterns
for stories and poems and sentences and words.
These patterns enter through the ear
and remain available throughout the course of a lifetime
for reading and writing and speaking.
The good reader is a person who looks at a page of print
and begins triggering patterns
that have been stored in his linguistic treasury.
These patterns range all the way
from the plot structure an author has used in a story
to the rhyme scheme that hangs a poem together,
to the placement of an adjective in front of a noun
as part of the shape of a sentence,
to the underlying rhythmical structure in a line of prose or poetry,
to the *ed* ending as part of the shape of a word.

As these various kinds of structures
are brought into play
as a result of encountering a new version
of the same old basic structure,
a child is able to figure out much of the new vocabulary
because he recognizes the similarity
between the new structure
and structures he has already claimed.
A poor reader is the person who looks at a page of print
and no patterns are triggered to help him unlock the page.
This can be because he has not been read or talked to very much
and therefore has not deposited
story and poem and sentence and word patterns
in his linguistic storehouse.
Or this lack of triggering can occur
even if he has been talked to a lot
if the oral language patterns are not the kind
he is encountering in print.
A Spanish-speaking child, for example,
has stored sentence patterns
where the adjective follows the noun.
This does not help him unlock English sentences
where the adjective precedes the noun.
He will first have to hear and store in his being
the typical shape of English sentences
before his linguistic storehouse can help him unlock English print.

Now you can see why reading aloud
the poems and stories in the *Sounds of Language* readers
is a continuing part of this reading program
for children of all ages throughout their school years.
Sometimes you are reading aloud and the children are listening,
sometimes you are reading aloud and the children are chiming in,
sometimes the children are reading in chorus,
sometimes the boys and girls are reading aloud in dialogue,
sometimes the children are chorusing a poem or story by memory,
sometimes you and the children are reading aloud together,
with the children following the print in their books
so their eyes can be seeing what their ears are hearing
what their tongues are saying.

Reading Aloud to Deposit Literary and Linguistic Structures TE 17

Dust
of Snow

The   way a crow
Shook down on me
The dust of snow
From a hemlock tree

Has given my heart
A change of mood
And saved some part
Of a day I had rued.

—"Dust of Snow" by Robert Frost, from *Sounds of a Young Hunter*

For example, a child who has heard frequently
and later read and chorused aloud "Dust of Snow,"
will have deposited within his linguistic treasury
a feeling for the sound and meaning of the word *rued*
that enhances his potential use of the word
in all kinds of communication—
reading, writing, speaking and listening.
He also will have a reservoir of potential
for shaping a sentence with the expertise
of this sentence shaped by a poet.
There is no better way for children to learn
to appreciate and use our language
than having broad and continuous experiences
that attune both the ear and the tongue—then later the eye—
to the rhythms, melodies and sounds of language.

Hopefully this reading aloud and language consolidation
will be accompanied by spontaneous body movement—
either the kind of swaying and clapping and shuffling
that children initiate on their own
or interesting movements suggested by you.
Whenever children engage their entire bodies
in their responses to print,
they have the best possible chance
to bring wholeness to the reading act
and intaking linguistic know-how.

3 INNOVATING ON LITERARY STRUCTURE TO CLAIM BASIC PATTERNS

One choice in deciding how to follow-up
your reading aloud of a story or poem
is to invite the children to utilize the author's pattern
for expressing their own thoughts.
By borrowing the underlying structure
of a poem or story or sentence that they have come to know,
they·are involved in two linguistically sound learnings
as they hang their own ideas on that structure:

1) they are having intuitive experiences
   with the fact that stories and poems
   do have underlying structures,

2) they are building a bridge between
   the linguistic facts of their worlds
   and the linguistic facts of the printed page.

The invitation to "Write about anything you want to"
may fall heavily on the ears of a child
who doesn't own the basic language structures
to give wings to what he wants to say.

On the other hand, a child of seemingly meager vocabulary
can latch onto a structure that comes in through his ears
and deposits itself indelibly in his mind,
and suddenly find his vocabulary taking on new strength.

Christmas 1969

And lo it came to be
that she bore an infant
in the subway. Because
the apartment cost was
too high. She wrapped
him in paper towels
from a gas station. And
lay him on the cold walk-
way. The train rattled
by but no sound came
from him.

And it came to be
that friends heard of him
and came to see him.
They brought with them
gifts of grape drink, cigar-
ettes, and a few dollars.

—Kevin Clark, grade 6, Issaquah Valley School, Issaquah, Washington.

The *Sounds of Language* readers
make it possible for children of either rich or meager vocabulary
to find challenge in their new creations which come about
as they innovate on the dependable structures found in these books.
Your reading table may come alive
with fifteen new books (written by children)
each time you read a story or poem
and invite the children to borrow the structure
and to adorn it with their own thoughts and language.
What a wonderful source of material the reading table becomes
for the children's independent reading.
Since all of the innovative books
are built on structures which the children have already claimed
in read-aloud times with the *Sounds of Language* books,
the children will not only be able to read the new books more easily,
but they will be recognizing how useful

a person's knowledge about underlying structure
can be in helping him read.
Thus, children who have just finished reading:

Good night, Mr. Beetle,
Good night, Mr. Fly,
Good night, Mrs. Ladybug,
The moon's in the sky.

Good night, Miss Kitten,
Good night, Mr. Pup,
I'll see you in the morning
When the sun comes up.

—Sounds of Home

will tend to feel that they are meeting
an old friend when they come upon a child's innovated story:

Merry Christmas, Mr. Beetle,
Merry Christmas, Mr. Fly,
Merry Christmas, Mrs. Lady Bug,
Santa's in the sky.

Merry Christmas, Miss Kitten,
Merry Christmas, Mr. Pup,
I'll see you Christmas morning
When I open presents up.

Once the children have latched on to this notion
of borrowing a favorite literary structure for their own creations,
you will have many surprises in store.
Suddenly all of children's linguistic storehouse treasures
become available to them—
structures they have claimed both in and out of school—
and they begin to appear in the children's writing.
Imagine the surprise and delight of a fifth-grade teacher
who had asked his children to do a piece of writing
that would cause him to see pictures,
when a boy who had been considered an academic dropout
came up with this piece of writing:

The Frog

The frog in the pond a lony *(lonely)*
little fellow who lives with
the pussy wilow and the muss *(moss)*
who sits on a lilly like a bud wathing *(watching)*
the ixcitment of the day
when he sees a giant much bigger
than his size. He sits riady
coilled like a spring with bright
marrbled eys ready to dive
in the water and hid *(hide)* only to
disapear like mggic *(magic)* disgased *(disguised)*
with the polution of a once
lively and active pond.

—from Mr. Bredahl's sixth grade,
Roosevelt School, Minot, North Dakota

Where did the writing come from?
It has the ring of a poet,
yet the child obviously didn't copy it from print
for a poet would have grouped the words
into spoken speech units which this writing partially lacks.
Is this something this child heard
and deposited whole in his linguistic storehouse
and is now utilizing?
Or is it a combination of his own phrasing
and literary language he has stored?
The miracle is how beautifully and accurately
this boy has called upon his language storehouse
to fulfill his class assignment.
Luckily, this teacher did not feel
that it was *cheating* or *copying* or *uncreative*
to borrow literary lines and/or structure.
This is how a newcomer creates a language of depth and beauty.
Gradually he will transform and in other ways reshape
the language he has borrowed.
Meanwhile, in his borrowing,
he is role-playing himself as a distinguished user of language
and is tuning his ears to the beauty of speech.

Bruce's teacher experienced all of the wonder and surprise
of a genuine literary encounter
when she discovered these lines he had written:

Mystery of Bill Martin
True blue surprise rubbed over man's flat eyes
Truthful innocence scattered down Skinny's rectangular nose
—from Tucson Public Schools, class and grade unknown

Obviously Bruce has a well-stocked linguistic storehouse
and in self-selected ways he is experimenting
with combinations of words that please him,
albeit the sentence meanings are obtuse.

4 FIGURING OUT HOW STORIES AND POEMS WORK

Children like to figure out how things work.
From their earliest days
they are endlessly poking and pushing and pulling-apart
to find out what makes things go.
This is how they learned to talk.
They listened to the talk on all sides of them
and they began experimenting and figuring out how talk works.
Once they began to figure out what they needed to know,
they made talk work for them.

In a similar way,
when you read a highly structured story to children,
they will chime in with you long before you have finished the story:

Brown bear, brown bear,

what do you see?

I see a redbird

looking at me.

Redbird, redbird,

what do you see?

                I see a yellow duck

                looking at me. [1]

As you turn the page and the children burst out reading

Yellow duck, yellow duck,

what do you see?

knowing, without even looking at the print, how the story is working,
they are giving evidence
that they have not simply memorized the story.
They have figured out how the author put his story together
and they are using this information
to help them read pages you haven't even read to them yet.
Much of this kind of figuring-out is intuitive.
It goes on while you are reading aloud
and while the children are chiming the story along with you.
Your job is to help the children verbalize these intuitive insights
and to organize them into word-unlocking skills.
Knowing how stories and poems are put together
will therefore be a help both to you and the children.
To begin with, stories are a series of episodes
or happenings arranged in some kind of recognizable shape.
For our purposes we view an episode
as either an action within a series of actions
or a language pattern within a series of related language patterns.
In so far as possible, in designing the early *Sounds of Language* readers,
we have used the turning of the page to indicate a new episode.

[1] This story by Bill Martin appears
both in the *Kin/der Owls* and in the Level 1 *Instant Readers*.

In some stories, the episodes repeat one another.
We have called that kind of story structure *repetitive sequence*.

My name is Tommy.
I am not very big.

I am not as big as a goat.　　EPISODE 1
A goat is bigger than I am.

I am not as big as a horse.　　EPISODE 2
A horse is bigger than I am.

I am not as big as an elephant.　EPISODE 3
An elephant is bigger than I am.

I am not as big as a whale.　　EPISODE 4
A whale is bigger than I am.

I am not as big as a dinosaur.

EPISODE 5

A dinosaur is the

biggest thing I know.

—from "What Is Big?" *Sounds of Numbers*

Even on first acquaintance, a child will predict

1) that the pattern of phrasing will maintain,

2) that all of the creatures will be described as big/bigger,

3) that in each comparison, the last part of the first sentence becomes the first part of the second sentence.

When the children come to the last episode, numbered 5,
and the repetitive pattern breaks,
we have dramatically enlarged the new language pattern
to signal to the children that something has changed
and the repetition has stopped.
The enlarged type also is a semantic clue
that tends to trigger children
into use of the superlative form of the adjective *big*,
which in its own way
also signals the end of the comparative sequence.
These kinds of exaggerated clues help children learn to trust print,
knowing that an author will keep leaving visual clues
that help the reader decode.
Imagine a child's surprise, therefore,
to discover that the dinosaur is not *bigger than I am*
but is *the biggest thing I know.*
Couched as this variation is within so many dependable repetitions,
it does not cause a child to lose faith in structural repetitions,
but rather it invites him to develop another literary insight—
that when a repetitive pattern gets going,
the author will at some time break the pattern
in order to bring the story to an end.
His curiosity is, therefore, piqued
to predict ways the author can break a repetitive pattern.

Let's look at another example:

Round is a pancake,   EPISODE 1
Round is a plum,   EPISODE 2
Round is a doughnut,   EPISODE 3
Round is a drum.   EPISODE 4

Round is a puppy   EPISODE 5
    Curled up on a rug.
Round are the spots   EPISODE 6
    On a wee ladybug.

Here is the pattern break signalling that the story is ending.

Look all around,   EPISODE 7
On the ground, in the air,
You will find round things
Everywhere.

—from *Sounds of Home*

Although episodes 5 and 6 are patterned extensions
of the previous episodes,
the reliability of their beginning phrases
cues the children to predict
that they can make a go
of a somewhat different sentence.
And, when the children come to the last episode, number 7,
and it does not begin with the repeated phrase *Round is*,
they have a reliable clue for predicting
that this repetitive story is coming to an end.

And here's a repetitive pattern
that's worn smooth with a lifetime of continuations:

As wet as a 🐟 — as dry as a bone;

As live as a bird — as dead as a stone;

As plump as a partridge — as poor as a rat;

As strong as a 🐴 — as weak as a 🐱 ;

As hard as a flint — as soft as a mole;

As white as a lily — as black as a coal;

As plain as a staff — as rough as a 🐻 ;

As tight as a 🥁 — as free as the air;

As heavy as lead — as light as a 🪶 ;

As steady as time — as uncertain as weather;

As hot as an oven — as cold as a 🐸 ;

As gay as a lark — as sick as a 🐕 ;

As savage as tigers — as mild as a dove;

As stiff as a poker — as limp as a 🧤 ;

As blind as a bat — as deaf as a post;

As cool as a 🥒 — as warm as toast;

As blunt as a 🔨 — as sharp as an awl;

As flat as a flounder — as round as a ⚾ ;

As brittle as glass — as tough as gristle;

As neat as a pin — as clean as a 🧢 ;

As red as a 🌹 — as square as a box;

As bold as a thief — as sly as a 🦊 .

—from *Sounds of Mystery*

While most stories have more than one kind of pattern
in their make-up,
many of the *Sounds of Language* selections
have enough obvious repetitions in their underlying structures
that children are propelled into anticipating the next line or episode.
Naturally this is not an infallible method
of decoding print,
but it is highly useful in combination with
the many other decoding skills
which are developed in the *Sounds of Language* program.
Moreover, it releases children to a continuous flow of reading
without the traditional vocabulary breakdowns
that are engendered by word-by-word reading
and which rob the language of its melodies and structural rhythms.
Children enjoy the *aha!* feeling which comes
when they predict that the second and third billy goats[2]
will behave much the same as the first billy goat
and when they predict that much of the language (and action)
in the first episode will be repeated.
They feel that they have a successful hold on the story
in "The Three Little Pigs and the Ogre"[3]

when the first little pig outwits the ogre
and they predict that the other two pigs
will try to do the same.
When children make identification with a strong character,
such as Ol' Stormalong,[4] they will predict
that even when he turns into a cowboy and a farmer,
much of his talk and actions
will repeat the talk and actions of Ol' Stormalong, the sailor.
Once you are aware
that a repetitive sequence is one way
of arranging the happenings in a story,
you probably will think of many other stories
which are arranged in this style.
You probably will also remember
how easily the children were able
to take hold of those stories
when you read them aloud.
At the time, you may not have realized
that the children were not simply memorizing—
that they were responding to the reliable repetition
in the story structure.

"Blo-o-ows!
Thar she blows!"

Swoosh!

"Hooray, a storm!" shouted Stormalong to the farmers.
"Now I can get the kinks out of my muscles.
Avast there, mateys! Storm ahead! All hands on deck!"

"Just sit down and rest yourselves,
me hearties," said Stormalong.
"I'll round 'em up,
just to get the kinks out of my muscles."

[2] "The Three Billy Goats Gruff," *Sounds of Laughter*

[3] *Sounds of Mystery*

[4] "How Ol' Stormalong Captured Mocha Dick," *Sounds of a Distant Drum*

Figuring Out How Stories and Poems Work TE 31

This is the house
    that Jack built.
This is the malt,
That lay in the house
    that Jack built.
This is the RAT
That ate the malt,
That lay in the house
    that Jack built.

—from *Sounds Around the Clock*

How pleasantly this old cumulative rhyme
falls into place.
Each new line (episode) adds a new thought
before repeating everything that went before.
Children who sense the cumulative nature of this story
have a lot going for them.
They know, for example, that all of each subsequent page
will be familiar to them
except for the one added thought.
They also know that each new page will have more type
than the preceding page
and that they will be able to easily read
this accumulating language because it is familiar.
Children, on the other hand,
who are taught to read word by word,
are often turned away from pages with a lot of type
because they do not have structural insights
to help them unravel the print.

Throughout *Sounds of Language* children will encounter
stories and poems and songs and jingles
put together with a cumulative structure.
Each new encounter will remind them
that their insight into new selections
is influenced by the fact
that the basic pattern of cumulative writing
has already been deposited in their linguistic storehouses
and is now available for a lifetime of use
in reading and writing and literary appreciation.

Just for fun, let's see at which point you sense
that "I Came to this Land"
is cumulative in structure.

> *When I first came to this land,*
>> *I was not a wealthy man,*
> *Then I built myself a shack.*
>> *I did what I could.*
> *I called my shack, Break-my-back.*
> *Still the land was sweet and good,*
>> *I did what I could.*
>
> *When I first came to this land,*
>> *I was not a wealthy man,*
> *Then I bought myself a cow.*
>> *I did what I could.*
> *I called my cow, No-milk-now,*
> *I called my shack, Break-my-back.*
> *Still the land was sweet and good.*
>> *I did what I could.*
>
> —from "I Came to this Land," *Sounds Jubilee*

Up until the line in the second verse,
"*I called my shack, Break-my-back,*"
this structure obviously is repetitive,
but the use of this particular line in sequence with the new episode
is evidence for predicting
that this is both a repetitive and cumulative sequence,
and that each new episode will include
an accumulation of the man's previously named possessions.

Thus, you can figure out all six verses of this story song
with just the following information:

> *I bought myself a horse,*
> *I called my horse, Lame-of-course.*
>
> *I bought myself a duck,*
> *I called my duck, Out-of-luck.*

Aha! Now you're sensing that each creature's given name
is rhyming with the categorical name of the creature—
another structural clue.
Now you have three kinds of literary structure
going for you—repetitive, cumulative and rhyme-rhythm.

> *I got myself a wife,*
> *I called my wife, Joy-of-life.*
>
> *I got myself a son,*
> *I told my son, "My work's done."*

Aha! The author now has broken the language repetition,
signalling that he has probably reached the conclusion of his story.
Observe the additional semantic shift
in the first word of the last chorus:

> ***For*** *the land was sweet and good,*
> *I did what I could.*

This indeed confirms the fact that the story is over.
Did you enjoy getting hold of the story
partly by recognizing how the author put it together?
That same *aha!* feeling of awareness
that came to you as you figured out the pattern
and then made the pattern help you read the story successfully
is the same feeling that children get
when they sense an author's plan.
At the end of this section on various types of literary structure,
you'll find suggestions
for helping children verbalize the *aha!* feeling
and developing it into a word-unlocking skill.

C) Interlocking Sequence

Sometimes the episodes in a story or poem or song
do not simply repeat or accumulate,
rather they interlock in an intriguing way.

> *The funny old man and the funny old woman*
> *sat by the fire one night.*
> *"Funny old man," the old woman said,*
> *"I don't know what to do.*
> *When I went to the barn to milk the cow,*
> *the funny old cow wouldn't moo."*
>
> *The funny old man scratched his head,*
> *"I know what to do," he said.*
> *"Take her to town to see Dr. Brown*
> *and bring her home in the morning.*
> *That's what you do when the cow won't moo."*
>
> *"But she's out in the woodshed lying down.*
> *How will you take the cow to town*
> *and bring her home in the morning?"*
>
> *"If she can't walk," said the funny old man,*
> *"I'll push her in the wheelbarrow if I can*
> *and bring her home in the morning."*
>
> *"But the goat's asleep in the wheelbarrow.*
> *Where shall I put the goat?"*
>
> *"Put the goat on top of the garden gate.*
> *The goat can sleep there very late*
> *till the cow comes home in the morning."*
>
> *"But the rooster is roosting on the garden gate.*
> *Where shall I put the rooster?"*
>
> *"Put the rooster in the butter churn,*
> *so tight that he can't twist or turn*
> *till the cow comes home in the morning."*
>
> *"But ..."*

—from "The Funny Old Man and the Funny Old Woman,"
Sounds of Laughter

Are you caught up in the intrigue
of this sequence, and ready to predict the

> "But..." (says the old woman)

> "Put..." (says the old man)

pattern on which this story is built?

Even if you had never learned
to sound out the word *butter*,
you are prepared to read this word in this story slot

> "But my nice fresh butter is in the churn.

> Where shall I put my butter?"

knowing how it interlocks with the preceding lines

> "Put the rooster in the butter churn

> so tight that he can't twist or turn

> till the cow comes home in the morning."

Finally in this humorous story
when the old man says,

> "Put the pig on a pillow in the feather bed,"

and the old woman says,

> "No,"

instead of

> "But,"

you know for sure that the interlocking pattern has been broken
and the story is coming to an end.

Now to exploit your structural know-how,
have a go at this:

I came to the river...

and I couldn't get across,

I jumped on a frog 'cause I thought it was a hoss,

The hoss wouldn't pull so I traded for a bull,

The bull wouldn't holler so I sold him for a dollar,

The dollar wouldn't pass so I threw it in the grass,

The grass wouldn't grow so I traded for a hoe,

The hoe wouldn't dig so I traded for a pig,

_ __ __ squeal _ _ __ _ _ wheel,

_ __ __ run _ _ __ _ _ gun,

_ __ __ shoot _ _ __ _ _ boot,

_ __ __ fit _ _ thought I'd quit

And I did.

—an old rhyme, Sounds of Mystery

Think how much vocabulary is unlocked
simply by recognizing that these lines
interlock with one another
rather than simply follow one another.
You probably remember adult stories
where some happening triggered off
or brought together a chain of events,
such as in *The Bridge at San Luis Rey*
or Chaucer's *Canterbury Tales.*
Even the reading or viewing of Shakespearean plays
is both simplified and intensified
when you recognize the interlocking relationships
of characters.
The moment you con Lady Macbeth
or Claudius or Petruccio, for example,
you begin predicting events and language.
What a reading skill!

D) Familiar Cultural Sequences

Simply by living in our culture,
children have certain built-in structures going for them
that can be put to work in learning to read.
They know, for example, that the hours of the day,
the days of the week, the months and seasons,
the number system and the alphabet
have dependable sequences.
Sooner or later
children become familiar with and use these sequences
like another hand or foot or ear or eye
in dealing with the outside world.
The *Sounds of Language* program
exploits certain of these structures
as another way to help children appreciate the fact
that the recognition of underlying sequence
is an aid in decoding print:

In the first month of the year
I found one brown pony
and he followed me home.

In the second month of the year
I found two white kittens
and they followed me home.

—from "One, Two, Three, Four," Sounds of Numbers

Children are now prepared to read the words *third* and *three*
because they sense that along with the repetition
in this story
is a reliance on ordinal and cardinal numbers.
Similarly,

On Monday I make strong boxes ...

   On Tuesday

   I make

   narrow boxes ...

—from "A Maker of Boxes," Sounds of Laughter

children who have never seen the word *Wednesday*
anticipate that it will be used in the next episode,
and will read the word in its appropriate slot,
confirming the fact that they recognize
the author's basic way of organizing his story.
It's a proud triumph for a reader.

Seventh graders can enjoy unlocking print
by using a familiar cultural sequence (the alphabet)
that has been with them since nursery school days:

A you're adorable, B
you're so beautiful, C you're a
cutie full o' charms D you're a
darling, and E you're exciting,
and F you're a feather in my arms.

—from "A You're Adorable," *Sounds Jubilee*

Once you and the children recognize familiar cultural sequence
as the organizing factor in putting certain stories together,
you may wish to begin a bulletin-board collection
of such sequences.
And don't be surprised if the children list the count-down
as a sequence which is securely deposited
in their linguistic storehouses.

Sometimes it is easy to hunch early in a story
that the episodes are arranged chronologically.
This kind of hunch gives the expectation
that the vocabulary will be influenced
by an ordering of events based on time.
Biographies and autobiographies
tend to work this way.
Very often detective stories
unfold in a time sequence.
Even in the old nursery rhyme when

>   *Jack and Jill went **up** the hill*

you expect them to come tumbling *down*.

Children are in the mood
for spanning the events of a lifetime
when they read:

> This is Johnny.
>
> He is a baby.
>
> He cannot walk.
>
> He cannot talk.
>
> But he can cry!
>
> Johnny is 1 week old.
>
> Now Johnny can walk.
>
> He laughs and claps his hands.
>
> He says "dada" and "mama"
> and "baby."
>
> Johnny is 1 year old.

Now Johnny is 4 years old. . . .

He is not a baby anymore. . . .

Johnny is 6 years old now

He is in the first grade. . . .

Now Johnny is 12.

He goes to junior high school. . . .

—from "Growing Up, Growing Older,"
Sounds of Laughter

As children follow Johnny's life
through to his happy grandfather days,
they anticipate and soon are comfortable with lifetime words
such as *junior high school, young man, college,
home from the air force, wedding day.*
Even as they study the art for clues,
children have strong notions of what they are looking for
(such as signs of physical aging, and signs of maturity)
because of their recognition
of the chronological sequence on which the story hangs.

In even wider ranging applications
of this particular literary know-how,
children will create useful expectations
based on other kinds of chronological sequencing:

1) the logical ordering of events in a story,
   particularly a mystery story where the solution
   usually comes at the end:
   such as "The Ghostly Hitchhiker,"
   Sounds Freedomring

2) the ordering of events on a trip,
   be it a spaceflight or a picnic.

3) the shaping of events by weather patterns,
   i.e. "Snowbound," *Sounds of a Distant Drum*

4) explanatory sequences such as giving directions,
   i.e. "How to Brush Your Teeth," *Sounds of a Young Hunter*

F) Problem-Centered Sequence

The minute Mother Meadowlark awakens
with a snake curled about her nest,
there is no doubting that she has a problem.[5]
Whenever a main character in a story
is confronted with a crucial problem,
the person reading the story can predict
that one episode after another will occur
until the problem is solved.
Once the problem is solved
the reader does not expect the story to go on
for fifty more pages.
He knows that the story is finished.
There isn't that much more to talk about.
The episodes which occur in solving the problem
can be repetitive, cumulative,
interlocking or chronological.
They can also be arranged
around familiar cultural sequences.
In other words,
a story does not have only a basic shape.
It can also have shapes within shapes.
Children reading "The Billy Goats Gruff"[6]
soon recognize that the episodes which occur as the three goats
solve their problem with the troll
are repetitive.

[5] "Mother Meadowlark and Brother Snake," *Sounds of the Storyteller*
[6] *Sounds of Laughter*

The bridge goes,

"Trip, Trap! Trip, Trap! Trip, Trap!"

each time a goat crosses over.
The troll threatens each time.
The goats respond.
When the third goat breaks the repetitive pattern
and solves the problem,
the story comes to an end.
In their reading of the story,
children have two kinds of structural insight going for them:

1) the problem of the troll and its solution;

2) the repetition of action
   and vocabulary from episode to episode.

In "The Web of Winter"[7]
the main character encounters a problem
when he discovers a young duck unable to fly
because it is frozen in the ice.
From that point on, the episodes move chronologically.
As Bill frantically tries to free the bird
and the day moves toward night,
the children reading the story
are reaching out toward a solution.
And while the problem-centered, chronological structure
does not predict the exact language,
it does prepare the children to expect vocabulary
related to the efforts to save the duck,
to the actual saving of the duck,
to the passing time of day,
to the vocabulary associated with the passing time of day,
such as *suppertime, darkness, headlights*, etc.
and to certain character traits.
All of these linguistic insights
are germane to unlocking the print.

[7] *Sounds of Mystery*

Some poems and stories
are put together with a dependable rhyme-rhythm scheme.

The Owl and the Pussy-cat went to sea
In a beautiful pea-green boat:
They took some honey, and plenty of money
Wrapped up in a five-pound note.

—from "The Owl and the Pussy Cat," *Sounds After Dark*

You may have been taught
that this is an A-B-C-B rhyme-rhythm scheme,
meaning that the second and fourth lines rhyme
and the rhythm is predictable.
Heaven forbid that we lecture children
about the A-B-C-B rhyme-rhythm scheme!
But we can help them verbalize the fact
that when you have figured out
the author's rhyming-meter plan,
it is easier to read the rhyming words
and to syllabicate certain words
used in the rhyme-rhythm slots.

Slowly ticks the big clock;

Tick-tock, Tick-tock!

But Cuckoo clock ticks double quick;

Tick-a-tock-a, tick-a-tock-a,
Tick-a-tock-a, ☐ [8]

Do you find yourself supplying the word *tick*
to keep the rhyme scheme going?
This is how it is with response to rhyme scheme.

[8] "The Big Clock," *Sounds Around the Clock*

One way to help children verbalize
how useful a rhyme scheme can be
in recognizing vocabulary
is to read them a regularly patterned verse
and ask them to supply words you leave out.

> *Boys and girls, supposing you keep your books closed*
> *while I read you an old rhyme.*
> *I'm going to leave out some of the words*
> *and you see if you can say those words*
> *even though you've never heard the poem:*

This is the story

Of Susie Moriar.

It started one night

As she sat by the ☐

The fire was so hot,

Susie jumped in a ☐

The pot was so black,

Susie dropped in a ☐

The crack was so narrow,

Susie climbed on a wheel ☐

The wheelbarrow was so low,

Susie fell in the ☐

The snow was so white,

Susie stayed there all ☐

The night was so long,

Susie sang a ☐

—from "Susie Moriar," *Sounds of Laughter*

As the children supply the missing words,
they are responding to both the rhythmical and rhyming patterns
of this old jingle.
It is important to help them verbalize
their ways of figuring out the missing words
and to discuss the fact that
in their independent reading,
they can use this kind of structural insight
to figure out certain unknown vocabulary.
At some point in the discussion,
it can be useful to suggest:

> *Children, supposing you wanted*
> *to change the poem about Susie Moriar.*
> *Let's see where we can go with*
>
> *"This is the story of Jennie McGoo.*
> *It started one night as she . . ."*

As the children pick up the aa-bb-cc, etc. scheme
of the original jingle
they may be suggesting:

> *This is the story of Jennie McGoo.*
> *It started one night as she went to the zoo.*
> *The zoo was so bright,*
> *Jennie stayed there all night . . .*

Some children, however, may not respond
to the rhythm-rhyme scheme of the original jingle
and may come up with something like

> *This is the story of Jennie McGoo.*
> *It started one night as she went to sleep.*

When such a suggestion is made,
your role is to accept it positively
and help the children see the difference
between this and the original pattern.

Isn't this interesting, boys and girls?
Chuck has suggested a pattern
that doesn't rhyme the way the original poem did.
Let's follow Chuck's lead for awhile
and see where we go.

"This is the story of Jennie McGoo.
It started one night as she fell asleep.
Next thing she knew she was floating on a cloud . . ."

And so develops an innovation
that is patterned on story ideas
rather than the original rhyme scheme.
Both kinds of innovating are important.
As the children discuss differences
between rhyming and non-rhyming patterns,
they will further appreciate how recognition
of a rhythm-rhyme scheme
helps a person unlock unknown vocabulary.

Obviously there are other and more subtle literary structures
such as a story like "Old Lucy Lindy"[9]
and "Yallery Brown"[10]
in which the episodes hang on character development
but for purposes of this discussion
we have confined ourselves to those story patterns
which are most productive
in helping children predict language
and thereby unlock vocabulary.

In all of this discussion
of ways for putting stories and poems together,
we have been faced with the interesting fact
that whenever many of anything come together,
be they objects or events or words or people,
they either fall together helter-skelter
or they fall into an arrangement of some kind.
An earthquake produces hit-and-miss.
Language, whatever else, creates order.

[9] *Sounds of the Storyteller*
[10] *Sounds Freedomring*

When children are helped to verbalize
their recognition of the various ways
authors can arrange episodes in a story or poem,
they develop a reading skill
that forever lifts them out of the
little-steps-for-little-feet way of viewing a book.
A book or story or poem, whatever else it is,
is not a succession of isolated words
to be sounded out
or an unmanageable succession
of disassociated thoughts and events.
Traditional "basic" reading and language instructions
are not "basic" in the least
unless they include opportunities
for children to develop their naturalistic and intuitive skills
in unlocking the flow of language
in its basic cultural patterns.
It's as important for a child to know
how a piece of writing is unfolding
as it is for him to know
how a word unlocks.
The joyful fact is
that as a child takes root and strength
in his abilities to anticipate literary structure,
he, simultaneously, is developing word-unlocking skills
that save him from being stranded
with "sounding out" as the only way
to manage unknown words.

Figuring Out How Stories and Poems Work TE 49

5 HELPING CHILDREN VERBALIZE THEIR INTUITIVE LITERARY INSIGHTS

You may be wondering
how to help children
verbalize their structural insights.
Actually, your discussion with the children
occurs all along the line.

If the children quickly chime in
during your first reading of a story,
you may wish to engage them in easy conversation
about their ease in chiming in.

> *How come you children were able to read
> so much of that story
> without hearing it first?*

Their homely explanations will tell you
whether or not they are using
the structure of the story
as one of their ways for unlocking print.

> *When he said, "I'm not as big as a goat"
> and "I'm not as big as a horse,"
> I knew he was going to keep on saying
> "I'm not as big as a . . . . ."*

This is a young child's natural way for telling you
that he is beginning to recognize repetitive sequence.

> *How does it happen you children
> read that word* Wednesday *so easily?*

> *"Well, when the author said
> 'On Monday I build . . .' and
> then when he said, 'On Tuesday
> I build . . .' I knew he was going
> to say, 'On Wednesday . . .' "*

Here a child is verbalizing his awareness
of structure built on familiar cultural sequences.

> *Isn't it interesting, children,*
> *when you figure out how an*
> *author put his story together,*
> *it helps you in your reading.*

This kind of remark will help children
generalize their experience in the use of literary structure
to unlock print.
It also helps give them the vocabulary
for verbalizing what they have experienced.
A word of caution:
generalizing statements of this kind do not come
before the children have had the experience
of successfully using story or poem structure
to make their reading easier.
If the generalizations are to be the children's—
and they must be the children's
if they are to become part
of their personal collection
of word-unlocking skills—
they must grow out of first-hand experiences.
When they do grow out of first-hand experiences,
the children will claim the generalizations as their own,
depositing them in their linguistic storehouses
for future reference.
If the children are reading independently
and can recognize words
with or without help from literary structure,
you may wish to come at your questioning
from a different angle.

> *Children, supposing you had never seen*
> *the word Wednesday (or any other word*
> *that can be anticipated*
> *by knowing the structural sequence of the story).*
> *Is there anything in this story*
> *that gives you a hint*
> *that could help you read the word?*

This kind of questioning may lead
to a full-blown inquiry
into the various ways stories and poems are put together.
The children may wish to collect and categorize
favorite stories and poems they have read in the past:
repetitive, cumulative, interlocking, familiar cultural sequences,
problem-centered, rhythm-rhyme scheme.
All of this activity should have the zestful spirit
of scientific inquiry.
The children's satisfaction will come
from really figuring out
how something in their world works.

If you are teaching older boys and girls
who have never had experiences
with this approach to word-unlocking,
you may wish to get hold of a set of *Instant Readers*.[11]
These Bill Martin books are written
around the basic literary structures
and the books are discussed from this point of view
in the Teachers Guide.
Because the books are short and the structures are exaggerated,
the children can analyze them more easily
than they can longer stories.
You can also use the earlier *Sounds of Language* readers
with older boys and girls
if you reassure them
that you are doing grown-up things with the books.
Once you get into analyzing the author's plan
for putting his story together,
the children will respect the use of the younger books.

[11] Holt, Rinehart and Winston Inc.

And don't forget to browse through
the *Sounds of Language* books provided
for your particular class.
In even the seventh and eighth grade anthologies
you will find numerous short selections
that lend themselves to obvious literary analysis.

You may have to remind yourself
that these books do not have to be read
page-by-page from cover to cover
as most other readers do.
You can pick and choose from anywhere in the book,
depending on the interests and purposes
of the children and yourself.
Neither do the selections have to be exploited
in a single lesson and then left as "finished."
You can return to favorite selections
dozens of times throughout the year
for different purposes.

> *Boys and girls, do you remember*
> *the story "Ming and Ling"*[12]
> *that we enjoyed so much?*
> *Let's take another look at it. This time . . .*

Who knows how many useful excursions
children can conduct
through a story or poem that has been deposited
in their linguistic storehouses.
This is the reason for depositing the literature—
to make it available for a lifetime
of analysis and pleasure.

[12] *Sounds Freedomring*

Some of the best opportunities
for analyzing literary structure will come
when the children are borrowing the author's pattern
and hanging their thoughts and vocabulary on it.

Boys and girls, let's take a look
at this rather simple story:

"I am not as big as a goat.
A goat is bigger than I am.

I am not as big as a horse.
A horse is bigger than I am.

I am not as big as an elephant.
An elephant is bigger than I am.

I am not as big as a whale.
A whale is bigger than I am.

I am not as big as a dinosaur.
A dinosaur is the biggest thing I know."

—from "What Is Big?" *Sounds of Numbers*

If you were to borrow
the author's exact pattern
and make your own story out of it,
what would be important to remember?
Do you think you can make
even a simple pattern like this
interesting to fourth graders?

The children will probably verbalize
that the author has a plan for repeating.
They will probably notice that the describing word *big*
is central to the language pattern.
They may comment on his way for breaking the pattern
to bring the story to a close.
They may comment that the creatures
keep growing larger.
Fourth graders have been known
to come up with innovations
on even simple structures
that give them pleasure.

I am not as bony as my sister.
My sister is bonier than I am.

I am not as bony as a fish.
A fish is bonier than I am.

I am not as bony as spareribs.
Spareribs are bonier than I am.

I am not as bony as a skeleton.
A skeleton is the boniest thing I know.

—from a fourth grader, Corbett School, Tucson, Arizona

A sixth grader chooses the pattern from "A Turkey Speaks"
in *Sounds of a Distant Drum* for his innovation.

Taco Speaks

I have never understood
why anyone would
roast the shell
buy the meat
chip the pickles
chop the lettuce
when they could
sit back
and call. . . . .

Chicken
Delight

—from Pueblo Gardens School
Tucson, Arizona

Gradually you can help the children generalize
that when they are reading on their own
it is a good idea to be curious
about how the author put his story together
and that once they get the *aha!* feeling,
meaning that they have caught on to his plan,
they will be partly prepared for the vocabulary
they will encounter,
and that their structural insight
is both a writing and a reading skill.

6 FIGURING OUT
HOW SENTENCES WORK

In the same sense
that a story has a shape
and a poem has a shape,
so does a sentence have a shape.
A speaker pauses, intones, gestures
to show how the words group together
and thereby reveal his meanings.
A writer uses punctuation
to help the reader see
how the words group together.

The concept of *shapes of sentences*
is somewhat implied
in our earlier discussion of *chunks of meaning*.
In speaking and writing,
words do not simply follow one another
in unrelated separateness.
They cluster together to form a chunk of meaning
and these chunks of meaning
are basic to the shape of a sentence.
Not only that.
These chunks of meaning within a sentence
do not simply follow one another in random style.
They form a pattern as they fall next to one another
and recognizing the pattern is helpful in decoding.
One additional facet in the shaping of a sentence
is the fact that there is a definite order
in which many individual words fall in English sentences.
A chunk of meaning about a pretty girl
will not reverse this culturally established order
and call her a *girl pretty*.

Let's take a closer look
at these three characteristics
that influence the shapes of sentences
and see what the implications are
for developing reading skills
that are not provided for in most reading programs.

A) Sentences Work in Chunks of Meaning

One useful way to help children understand
that chunks of meaning
are basic to the shape of a sentence,
is to read aloud a sentence from a familiar story
and ask the children to keep their books closed
and raise their hands each time
they hear a chunk of meaning:

So the little squeegy bug
followed Creepy the Caterpillar
to his home under the cattail leaf,
and soon was safe and warm,
away from the storm,
and he slept soundly
until morning.

—from "Little Squeegy Bug," *Sounds After Dark*

Remind the children that different people may hear
different chunks of meaning
so they will not be worried about right and wrong answers
when they enter into a later discussion
of where the various chunks begin and end.

At no time should a child feel embarrassed
over his selection of a chunk of meaning.
Even if he errs,
he will self-correct (the hallmark of an educated person)
when he becomes comfortable with this concept.
And by the way, if you should find yourself
selecting different chunks of meaning
from the ones we have indicated
in the sentence from "The Little Squeegy Bug,"
don't become alarmed.
Frequently more than one choice is possible.
The test is: *Does the selection of a particular chunk of meaning*
have integrity in and of itself,
and does it leave a complete chunk on either side of it?

Another useful way to help children latch on
to the chunks-of-meaning concept
is to compare the line-by-line text of a story
which is arranged in chunks of meaning
in a *Sounds of Language* reader
with a chapter in their social studies book or other textbook
where traditional paragraphing style is used
to shape sentences to rigid right-left hand margins
regardless of chunks of meaning.
On the opposite page is a pictorial comparison
of language in paragraph form
with language in chunks of meaning.
Which more readily invites your reading interest?
Since a chunk of meaning is a unit of sense,
the children may profit from discussing
whether or not breaking the sentences into units of sense
makes for more reader ease and understanding.
Accept any observations the children care to make.
Some children may be so accustomed
to the rigid right-left hand margins
that they actually find this newer page design more difficult at first.
Whatever their reactions,
this kind of comparing and free discussion
will further their understanding of the fact
that sentences work in chunks of meaning.

BLIZZARD HITS WESTERN STATES

AIR FORCE'S "OPERATION FEEDLIFT" BALKED BY CONTINUING BLIZZARD

CHICAGO, Jan. 20—One of the worst storms in memory hit Montana, eastern Washington, Utah, Nevada, Wyoming, Colorado and the Dakotas today in the form of blizzards, floods and bitter Arctic cold.

Some areas were buried under as much as 80 inches of snow, which forced the closing of schools and blocked highways. Freezing winds blew roofs off buildings, smashed windows and ripped down power and telephone lines. Brief gusts of the blizzard winds reached speeds as high as 95 miles an hour in parts of Montana and the Dakotas.

CHICAGO, Jan. 20—
One of the worst storms in memory
hit Montana,
eastern Washington,
Utah,
Nevada,
Wyoming,
Colorado
and the Dakotas today
in the form of blizzards,
floods
and bitter Arctic cold.

Some areas were buried
under as much as
80 inches of snow,
which forced
the closing of schools
and blocked highways.
Freezing winds
blew roofs off buildings,
smashed windows
and ripped down
power and telephone lines.
Brief gusts of the blizzard winds
reached speeds
as high as
95 miles an hour
in parts of Montana
and the Dakotas.

—from *Sounds of a Distant Drum*

At some point in your figuring out how sentences work,
you will want to invite the children
to take a paragraph from a story or article
that is printed with the traditional right-hand margin
and break the sentences into chunks of meaning.
The markings may vary from child to child
but no marking should violate a unit of sense.
When variations do occur,
be sure to discuss the children's reasoning
back of their choices
to determine whether or not
a child is sensing the meaning
back of the clustering of words he has selected.

Somewhere during your discussion of ways
for breaking the rigid right-hand material
into chunks of meaning,
you will want to help the children verbalize the fact
that once they are able to break unbroken sentences
into chunks of meaning,
they are developing a skill
that will stand them in good stead
in their independent reading.
Gradually they will build the habit
of seeing chunks of meaning
whether or not the text has been printed that way.
This is germane to dealing
with the meaning encased in print.

You may wish to consider punctuation
while you are discussing chunks of meaning.
As a matter of fact,
this may be the first time
some of your children see the actual sense to punctuation.
They may have seen commas and periods
and all the rest
primarily as items to get right or wrong
as they fill in blanks in workbooks.
Now with this new look at the ways sentences work,
they may enjoy discussing
how punctuation came to be in the first place.

When man invented the code
that we call written language,
he immediately found the need
for additional inventions besides the letters
to make writing work.
He therefore invented periods and commas
and other signals
to help the reader hear
what the code was saying.
Won't it be interesting
if the children decide
that printing sentences
in chunks of meaning
can make
certain punctuation
unnecessary!

The pickety fence

The pickety fence
Give it a lick it's
The pickety fence
Give it a lick it's
A clickety fence
Give it a lick it's
A lickety fence
Give it a lick
Give it a lick
Give it a lick
With a rickety stick
Pickety
Pickety
Pickety
Pick

—by David McCord,
from *Sounds of a Young Hunter*

SOX SONG
RED SOX
BLUE SOX
WHITE SOX
GREEN SOX
BROWN SOX
BLACK SOX
COLORS·IN·BETWEEN SOX

—from *Sounds After Dark*

B) Sentences Work Because of WORD ORDER

One other characteristic of English sentences,
is the *order* in which individual words
are placed next to one another.
A three-year-old knows this.
He will say:

>   *Me hit you.*

It is true he is using
the incorrect form of the pronoun,
but he will not ruin the basic shape
of the sentence and say:

>   *Hit me you.*

He will not rearrange the usual word-order
and put the verb in front of the subject pronoun.
He will say

>   *big boy*

He will not say

>   *boy big*

He will not deny the fact
that in the English language
the adjective usually comes in front of the noun.
As a school child,
*if he is helped to experiment with sentences
and to verbalize his intuitive knowledge
about word-order in English sentences,*
he will partially unlock words
because of where they fall
and what function they perform in the sentence.
That child coming to this sentence, for example,

I found six spotted puppies.

will not sit and endlessly spit and sputter
over the *sp* sound in *spotted*
and then give up in despair if he can't sound out the word.

He will first of all recognize
that *spotted* is a describing word,
falling as it does, in front of *puppies.*
With this dependable structural clue,
he finds it useful to know that the word begins
with the *sp* sounds.
Knowing that the word describes *puppies*
narrows the range, as it were,
to the short array of culturally anticipated words
such as:

> *little puppies*
> *white puppies*
> *black puppies*
> *tiny puppies*
> *collie puppies*
> *friendly puppies*
> *hungry puppies*
> *spotted puppies*

Instead of being confronted with the whole wide world
of words at random
he now is seeking only an *sp* word that can appropriately
describe *puppies,*

> *spotted puppies.*

What a difference in psychological posture!
What a cultural reliability
that supports a child's best efforts!

In a different context,
a writer sometimes distorts natural *word order*
for emphasis on rhythm or dramatic effect
as Walter de la Mare does in this amazing sentence:

> All but blind
>> In his chambered hole
> Gropes for worms
>> The four-clawed Mole.

> —from "All But Blind," *Sounds of Mystery*

C) Sentences Work in Sequence Patterns

Another characteristic of English sentences
is the way in which
the various chunks of meaning
are connected with one another.
Interestingly enough,
these clusters of words
pattern in much the same way
that the episodes in a story pattern.

1) Repetitive Sequence

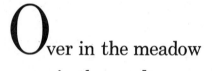

Over in the meadow

in the sand

in the sun

Lived an old mother turtle and her little turtle one.

—from "Over in the Meadow," *Sounds of a Powwow*

Repetition of chunks of meaning
is central to the shape
of this sentence.
Leave out *in the sand* and *in the sun*
and the basic design of the sentence
has been altered.
Once the basic designs for arranging sentences
have been deposited in the children's linguistic storehouses,
they own them for a lifetime of transforming
in their speaking and reading and writing.

2) Cumulative Sequence

Sometimes the chunks of meaning in a sentence
just keep adding on to one another
to give the sentence its shape.

Then, each monkey pulled off his cap...

and all the yellow caps...

and all the blue caps...

and all the red caps...

and all the polkadot caps...

came flying d o w n o u t of the tree.

—from "Caps for Sale," *Sounds of a Powwow*

Young children are great at writing cumulative sentences
once they discover the power in the little word *and.*
You've seen these sentences:

*I went home from school
and then I . . .
and then I . . .
and then I . . .
and then I . . .*

Instead of criticizing the children
in our well-intentioned effort
to get them to write more interesting sentences,
we should praise them for their discovery.

Julie, that's just about the longest sentence
I ever saw.
Did you know that all of your life
you'll be seeing and hearing sentences that are put
together that way? Let's take a look at your long sentence
and see if we can figure out how it goes together.
How did it get to be so long?

Accept any homely observations
the children care to make.

Well, I just kept saying
"and then, and then, and then . . ."

is a beginning verbalization
of the shape of a cumulative sentence.

If the children made observations
about the cumulative sequencing
from episode to episode in "The House that Jack Built,"
they may enjoy going back to the story now:

This is the COCK that crowed in the morn,

That waked the priest all shaven and shorn,

That married the man all tattered and torn,

That kissed the maiden all forlorn,

That milked the cow

    with the crumpled horn,

That tossed the dog, that worried the cat,

That killed the rat, That ate the malt,

That lay in the house that Jack built.

—from *Sounds Around the Clock*

Imagine what fun it will be to discover
that each new episode is actually a cumulative sentence.

In your discussion of the various ways
chunks of meaning are laid next to one another
in a sentence,
don't press for exact terminology.
Older boys and girls may enjoy some terminology
after they have explored the shapes of sentences (and stories)
but the most important part of the explorations
is their homely verbalizing of their self-selected observations
about the ways in which sentences work.

3) Interlocking Sequence

> Down by the river,
> Down by the river,
> Down by the river so green,
> Down by the river where daffodils grow,
> Down by the river where breezes blow,
> Down by the river where butterflies flit,
> That's where firefly lamps are lit.
>
> —from *Sounds I Remember*

Sometimes the chunks of meaning in sentences
do not simply repeat or add on.
They interlock with one another
(as the chunks do in the sample sentence here)
in ways that create the sentence form and meaning.
For the most part,
an interlocked sentence does not reveal its full meaning
until the last segment in the chain of interlocking.

Consider, for example,
how incomplete the meaning of the following sentence is
until the last segment hinges in:

> To the Sun
> Who has shone
> All day,
> To the Moon
> Who has gone
> Away,
> To the milk-white,
> Lily-white Star
> A fond goodnight
> Wherever you are.

—"Last Song," by James Guthrie,
Sounds of a Distant Drum

Did you notice the repetitive sequence of this sentence?
And also that the sentence maintains a simultaneous
repetitive and interlocking sequence.
Interestingly enough,
as you will observe in the two sample sentences given here,
the chunks of meaning in one
can be reordered (re-arranged) without destroying the meaning,
while in the other
the various chunks of meaning cannot be rearranged
without destroying both the shape and meaning of the sentence.
It is as if a cyclone came along
and stripped the sentence of its sense.
Of all the sentence patterns,
the interlocking sequence is perhaps the one
that best helps children understand
that sentences are not simply long strings of isolated words
hung together with a capital letter and a period.

Sentences, like stories,
are shapes within a shape.
They are chunks of meaning
which are laid next to one another
according to a design.
Recognizing the design
helps to unlock the meaning.

4) Chronological Sequence

Chronological sentences are probably the easiest
to figure out
in terms of recognizing their basic shape.
Everything moves ahead so orderly:

First, the

outside surface of your upper teeth; second, the

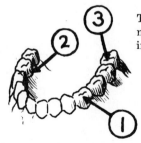

The same three areas of the lower teeth need careful cleaning: 1) outside, 2) inside, 3) biting edge.

inside surface of these teeth; third,

the grinding surfaces of the upper teeth.

—from "How to Brush Your Teeth," *Sounds of a Young Hunter*

Here's another sample:

> Then he reached up
>
> to make sure that they were straight—
>
> first his own striped cap,
>
> then the four yellow caps,
>
> then the four blue caps,
>
> then the four red caps,
>
> then on the very top the four polkadot caps.

—from "Caps for Sale," *Sounds of a Powwow*

And still another which is nonetheless chronological
because the time sequence is less obvious.

> So she (the Grandmarina)
> took it (the Magic Fishbone)
> from the hand of Princess Alicia
> and waved her magic fan over it,
> and it instantly flew
> down the throat
> of the dreadful little
> snapping pug dog next door
> and nearly choked him,
> and that was good!

—from "The Magic Fishbone," *Sounds Jubilee*

Once children sense that a sentence is moving forward
in chronological sequence,
they join right in with the author (anticipate)
in planning how the chunks of meaning will be arranged.

This kind of feeling that it is possible
to work one's way through a complicated looking sentence
because of recognizing its structure,
develops into a highly useful work-unlocking skill.

5) Rhyme-Rhythm Sequence

You can take a tub with a rub and a scrub

   in a two-foot tank of TIN,

You can stand and look at the whirling brook

   and think about jumping IN;

You can chatter and shake in the cold black lake,

   but the kind of bath for ME,

Is to take a dip from the side of a ship,

   in the trough of the rolling SEA.

—from "The Kind of a Bath for Me,"
Sounds of the Storyteller

This sentence moves forward
with a rhyme-rhythm sequence that helps give it its shape.
Children will readily recognize
that the intrigue and charm of the sentence
stem equally from the rhyme—
both internal and terminal— and from the rhythm.

In the following example, however,
it is the anticipation of rhyme, not rhythm,
that focuses the sentence sequence
and the unlocking of the word *precisely.*

. . . putting it my way, but nicely,

You are precisely my cup of tea!

—from "Getting to Know You," *Sounds of the Storyteller*

Here again, it's rhythm, not rhyme, that shapes a sentence:

Now, pray, where are you going?"
                    said Meet-on-the-Road.
"To school, sir, to school, sir,"
                    said Child-as-it-Stood.

—from "Meet on the Road," Sounds After Dark

Here is another sentence
so rhythmically shaped
that it stands alone like a poem:

ONCE IN THE GOLDEN TIME
    when an Irish king sat in every province
    and plenty covered the land,
there lived in Connaught
a grand old king with one daughter.

—from "The Princess and the Vagabond,"
Sounds of a Distant Drum

By clapping the rhythm of these sentences
and others that appeal,
children can develop sensitivity
to the rhythm of language,
a skill absolutely essential to anyone
who is to make a go of writing and reading.
You can, for example, invite someone to clap out a page of print
that all of the class has read frequently
to see if the selection can be recognized
solely by the linguistic rhythm.
At the same time
the children will be developing syllabication skills
in a far more functional setting
than looking a word up in a dictionary
for its stressed and unstressed patterns.

By clapping (and dancing) the rhythm of a sentence:

> I hoe and I plow
> I plow and I hoe
> And the wind drives over the main.
>
> I mow and I plant
> I plant and I mow
> While the sun burns hot on the plain.

—from "Farmer" by Liberty Hyde Bailey,
Sounds After Dark

the children will be getting the language
into their muscles as well as their minds,
a childhod naturality that makes language learning
pleasant and easy
until the pedants take over and deny children the use
of their basic language learning equipment.

Obviously there are other basic shapes to sentences
than the ones suggested in this essay,
but our purpose in this discussion is simply to alert you
that the clusters of words within a sentence
do fall together in various patterns
and that recognition of the pattern
is an aid in word-unlocking.
You may wish to jot down a few sentences from a favorite story
and see what observations you can make
about the patterns into which
the clusters of words fall.
First divide the sentences into their chunks of meaning
as we have done on these pages.
Then you are on your own.
Far more important than labeling the various shapes
is the recognition that sentences are not strings of words
which happen to fall together.

7 INNOVATING ON SENTENCE PATTERNS

By now you know
that when you read aloud to children
you are depositing various sentence patterns
in the children's linguistic storehouses
for a lifetime of use.
You probably are also aware
that when the children chime in on the reading,
especially in alive and dramatic ways
that include bodily movement,
they are themselves claiming and depositing these patterns.
One further activity
to help make these basic sentence structures
easily available to children for word-unlocking
in their reading and for writing and speaking,
is to invite them into systematic
and at the same time creative and lively experimenting
with the various patterns.
Here are four sentence manipulations
which have proved especially useful
for this kind of experimentation.

A) Transforming Sentences

Transforming a sentence
is the act of using the exact structure of a sentence
as the basis for creating a semantically new sentence
through either word-by-word substitution
or substitution of whole clusters of words.

> I   never   saw   a   purple   cow.
> —from *Sounds of Numbers*

Your first step in helping children transform this sentence,
after all of you have enjoyed reading the whole poem
from which it came,
is to copy the model sentence on the chalkboard,
leaving space between each word.
Then your conversation goes something like this:

> *Children, I'm going to draw a line*
> *to the word* cow.
> *Now, supposing we didn't want*
> *to use the word* cow.
> *What other words could we use*
> *instead of* cow?

Suggestions will begin to flow.

> I   never   saw   a   purple   cow.
> horse
> pig
> rabbit

Children, all of our naming words are animals.
Supposing we wanted another kind of naming word—
one that would make a spooky sentence.

> I   never   saw   a   purple   cow.
> horse
> pig
> rabbit
> spook
> vampire

Now, children, supposing we didn't want
to use the word purple?
Who else has a describing word?

Again the suggestions will flow.

I   never   saw   a   **purple**   **cow.**

brown	horse
pink	pig
hungry	rabbit
wailing	spook
	vampire

And so it goes until the children have suggested
vocabulary substitutions for all of the words.
You may wish to enter the game,
especially if the children are not having fun
with the substitutions they suggest.

Children, does anyone in this class
like silly sentences?
Well, I'm going to give you a new action word
that will really make a silly sentence.

I   never   **saw**   a   purple   cow.

kissed
loved
hugged
milked
married

Now the lid is off and the children's merriment
knows no bounds as they contemplate kissing purple vampires
and marrying pink spooks.
You may wish to invite the children

to go back to their tables
to write sentences of their choice.
At some point you may wish
to begin gentle conversation
about the word order in the sentence.

> *Isn't it interesting, children,*
> *that we don't say:*
>
> **I never saw a cow purple.**
>
> *I wonder why not.*

The children will probably suggest
that it just doesn't sound good—
meaning that their ears have already picked up
the usual word order in English sentences.
Gradually these kinds of conversations
help children add information
to their growing notions about how sentences work.
The *Sounds of Language* readers abound
in useful sentence patterns for the children to transform.
We have annotated a few of these sentences
to get you and the children started.
No attempt has been made to annotate every sentence
that lend itself to this kind of language analysis.
The peak value of the activity will come
when you and the children learn to go over a story
after enjoying it in its wholeness,
perusing it for *model sentences* rich in analysis potential.
It is your and the children's own selection
and manipulation of *model sentences*
that firmly connects the language learnings
with a child's personal use of language.
This is a qualitatively different learning experience
from that of filling in little blanks
in typical language workbooks.

Imagine what fun you and the children will have
when you select an intriguing sentence like this one
from E. B. White's *Charlotte's Web*
as a model to transform:

He	felt	the	pleasant	rubbing	of	the	stick

The
Wilbur	liked		brisk	prodding	in	those	rain
pig	heard		soothing	scraping	on	these	boys
She	wanted		incessant	dripping	after	a	enemy
man	hated		steady	yelling	under	an	goose
witch	ignored		heavy	knocking	over		doctor
farmer	fought		ugly	taunting	around		wheel
They				turning			motor
We				humming			
				throbbing			

Soon the children will be far-ranging in their choices
of serious and silly sentences offered by the framework:

They   hated   the   incessant dripping of   the   rain

The witch dreamed of a heady ride   on her broomstick

The motor made a suspicious wheezing   during the night

From time to time, you yourself will want
to suggest a vocabulary substitution
such as *skeleton, ghost, ferocious, monotonous,*
knowing that one strong, colorful word
will result in a flurry of additional substitutions.
When children become deeply involved
in transforming activities,
there's never time for each of them to read aloud
all of their self-selected sentences.

along	his	itchy	back.
under	her	itchy	hayrack
over	their	rough	bridge
along	the	rusty	terrain
in	that	tired	drainpipe
on	our	trusty	fence
at		creaking	brow
above		sagging	bed
		saggy	ear

through   the   sagging   roof.

with her irritable cat.

of our scary escape.

> This offers an opportunity for them to write sentences
> that eventually they can read to one another.
> *You can also suggest to the children*
> *that they keep in their notebooks*
> *a list of model sentences that especially appeal to them*
> *for later transforming in their personal writing.*
> Awarenesses of this kind
> are a sound linguistic base for both reading and writing.

B) Expanding Sentences

Expanding sentences is another technique
for helping children become aware
of the shape of sentences
and for helping them develop this awareness
into reading and writing and speaking skill.
This sentence manipulation is exactly
what the term *expanding* connotes.
Any simple sentence can be expanded
by adding phrases, clauses or describing words.

> *Children, let's take a sentence*
> *from our old jingle, "Susie Moriar."*

This   **is**   **the**   story   of   Susie   Moriar.

> *Let's see if we can think of some describing words*
> *to put in front of* **Susie.**

This   **is**   **the**   story   of   Susie   Moriar.

    funny
    kind
    nice

> *Now let's think of some describing words*
> *to put in front of* **story.**

This   **is**   **the**   story   of   Susie   Moriar.

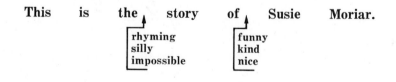

    rhyming   funny
    silly   kind
    impossible   nice

*Now who would like to try reading a sentence
using any of the words on the board?
Have you noticed, boys and girls,
how our sentence is getting longer and longer?
There is one other way we can expand this sentence
and make it even longer.
We can add a whole collection of words
that belong together.*

This   is   the   story   of   Susie   Moriar .

rhyming	funny	who lost her teeth
silly	kind	who likes to bake cakes
impossible	nice	who stands on her head

It's easy to see
that in writing the following sentence,
Anthony could have started with the simple statement:

The   king   was   old.

and then expanded it:

The King was so old
he could not dance the
twist so he said to
one of his girls to hold
him and do the twist
in slow motion.

—1st Grade, J. J. Ingalls School
Kansas City, Kansas

Older boys and girls search their linguistic storehouses
for single words and clusters of words
to make their sentence expanding worthwhile:

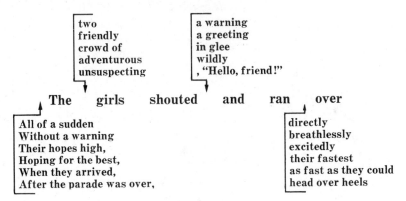

two
friendly
crowd of
adventurous
unsuspecting

a warning
a greeting
in glee
wildly
, "Hello, friend!"

The   girls   shouted   and   ran   over

All of a sudden
Without a warning
Their hopes high,
Hoping for the best,
When they arrived,
After the parade was over,

directly
breathlessly
excitedly
their fastest
as fast as they could
head over heels

An expanded sentence can be more dramatic,
"paint more pictures,"
or produce a more interesting array of sounds,
but it is not necessarily a better sentence.
In the process of expanding sentences, however,
children become keenly aware of the placement and function
of phrases and clauses and individual words
within a sentence.
And as they read their expanded sentences aloud,
they overtly are making judgments
about the kinds of sentences they do and do not like,
thus taking another step in the development of
and appreciation for a personal style
in writing and speaking.
It is this aware development
of a personal style
that helps children appreciate the fact
that authors of stories and poems
also have preferred styles.

```
                    ┌ new
                    │ old
                    │ big
                    │ open
                    │ dilapidated
                    │ comfortable
                    │ air-conditioned
                    └ well-lighted
                          ↓
to    Hippy Hippo's    cage ↑ .
                          ┌ nearby
                          │ in the arena
                          │ beyond the bridge
                          └ under the tree
```

—from "Hippy Hippo," *Sounds of Mystery*

A child with this kind of awareness
can browse through the first few pages
of a book he has selected from the library shelf
and make beginning judgments about the kinds of words
he will be unlocking simply by conning the author's sentence style.
If the sentences are involved
and packed with adjectives and adverbs,
this child will be sending signals to his linguistic storehouse,
as it were,
to trigger stored patterns to help with the reading ahead.

C) Transforming and Expanding Sentences

As children gain skill in sentence manipulations,
they will undoubtedly want to combine
two or more of the methods suggested here.
For example, colorful sentence possibilities emerge
when a model sentence is both transformed and expanded.
Consider the wide range of sentences
that is inherent in this diagram:

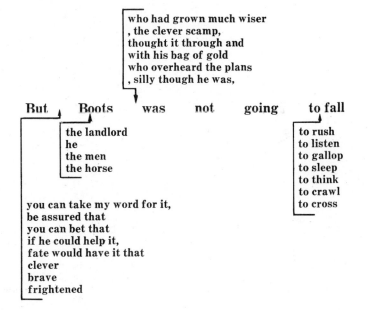

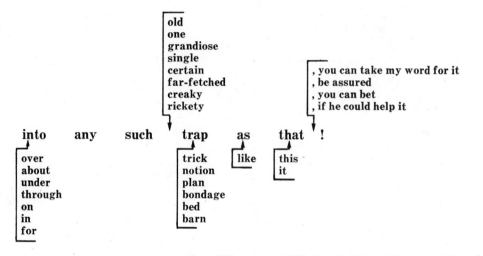

old
one
grandiose
single
certain
far-fetched
creaky
rickety

, you can take my word for it
, be assured
, you can bet
, if he could help it

into   any   such   trap   as   that !

over
about
under
through
on
in
for

trick
notion
plan
bondage
bed
barn

like

this
it

—from "How Boots Befooled the King," *Sounds of Mystery*

D)   Reducing Sentences

Another sentence manipulation
that is highly useful in helping children
figure out how sentences work
is reducing sentences.
When a person reduces a sentence,
he eliminates all unnecessary words, phrases and clauses.
The danger in reducing a sentence is that one is apt
to alter or destroy the sentence meaning
or to tamper with the author's style of writing.
As you and the children go through your *Sounds of Language* readers
in search of sentences to reduce,
you may have the same difficulty we had
when we searched for sentences to annotate for you.
The sentences are generally too well written for reducing.
However, in terms of children's learning,
the search is what is important.
As they consider which words or phrases or clauses
can or can't be eliminated,
they will be experimenting with the shapes of sentences
and will be storing their learnings for later use.
Now let's reduce a few sentences and analyze the results.

A bird ~~also~~ has another way to ~~help~~ keep ~~himself~~ warm in winter.

By seeing to it that ~~the~~ birds ~~near your home~~ have plenty to eat,
you can help "keep ~~their furnaces roaring"~~ and
their bodies warm in winter.

The bird's outer feathers
~~are staggered like shingles on a roof~~
~~to~~ keep out the rain and snow.

—from "How Birds Keep Warm in Winter," Sounds of Mystery

In the first sentence, the reducing sharpened the sentence.
The eliminated words are truly unnecessary.

In the second sentence,
the meaning is definitely altered by the deletions.
In the third sentence,
the question is not so much whether meaning has been altered
but whether the author's style has been tampered with.
As the children read Bernard Martin's article,
they will discover that here is an author
who paints pictures in the sentences he writes.
By eliminating such a vivid picture as
(feathers) *staggered like shingles on a roof,*
the sentence is rendered unimaginative,
albeit the sentence still makes its point
that the bird's feathers keep out the rain and snow.
One useful question to ask the children
after they have reduced an author's sentence is:

> *What do you think Bernard Martin*
> *would think about his sentence now?*

If they are referring to the third sentence above,
some children will probably conclude:

> *Well, he probably wouldn't like it very much.*

Then it can be profitable to look at other sentences
that suffer from being reduced.
The children may wish to turn
to a discussion of their own preferred sentence styles:

> *Jerry, would you say that you like best*
> *to write reduced or expanded sentences?*

More than one Jerry has been known to respond:

> *Well, I really like to write reduced sentences*
> *but you're always trying to get me*
> *to write expanded sentences.*

There are no right or wrong answers to these kinds
of linguistic inquiries.
Hopefully, the children will become versatile enough
to write and read many sentence styles.

Of one thing we are certain
from our observations in research classrooms
around the country:
children who have opportunities
to experiment with the shapes of sentences
will never again view reading as a matter
of sounding out isolated words.
They will not easily bog down or stop dead in their tracks
when they come to unknown words
because they will feel the strength of the language know-how
deposited in their linguistic storehouses
both in the form of literary and linguistic patterns
and in the form of worthwhile generalizations
about how language works
which they formulate in experimentation and discussion.

E) Rearranging Sentences

As we have already discussed,
ours is a word-order language.
The function of a word is highly dependent
on its position in the sentence.

> *I never saw a purple cow.*

A person who has listened to English sentences
all of his life, be he seven or seventy,
will hunch that the word *purple*
describes the word *cow,*
falling as it does directly in front of *cow.*
To change the word *the*
from first to second position in this sentence

> *The day is gone.*

destroys the meaning of the sentence
because the structure has been destroyed.
On the other hand,
the structure of some sentences
is not inflexible.

Jan came crying with her broken doll in hand.

can be significantly rearranged within the limitations
of our language system without a loss of meaning:

With her broken doll in hand, Jan came crying.
Jan came, with her broken doll in hand, crying.
Crying, with her broken doll in hand, came Jan.

Let's consider the sentence patterned on internal rhyme
which we enjoyed earlier in this discussion:

1) You can take a tub

2) with a rub

3) and a scrub

4) in a two-foot tank of tin.

This sentence can be easily rearranged 2-3-1-4
without destroying the structure or meaning.
You probably see other possibilities for rearranging,
while retaining the structure and meaning.
Consider the following sentence in the same light.
You readily can see multiple possibilities
for rearranging this sentence:

A truck came bumping
along the shore road,
its headlights shining
through the weeds.

—from "The Web of Winter," *Sounds of Mystery*

When you work with sentences this way on the chalkboard,
be sure to invite the children to make judgments
as to which arrangement they prefer.
This is germane to developing a personal style in writing,
for it is only by putting words together
in ways that are consistent with personality
that a person develops a *style* of writing.

Rearranging sentences is one of the many structural activities
that mark *Sounds of Language* as a comprehensive linguistic program.
Unlike some linguistic programs
that focus primarily on the shape of words,
Sounds of Language accepts realistically the fact
that the sentence is the basic unit of meaning in our language
and that an understanding of sentence structure
is basic to intaking sentence meaning.

Rearranging sentences best begins
with a recognition of the clusters of words
which are arranged in a particular way
to create the basic shape of the sentence.
Once a sentence has been divided into chunks of meaning,
a useful question is:

> *Children, do you see any clusters of words in this sentence*
> *which could be moved around?*

This awareness of movable parts in a sentence
helps children in reading long and difficult sentences.
Not only do they learn to read through it one chunk at a time,
but they also learn,
if a sentence has a difficult beginning,
to start reading the sentence at an easier point
and later pick up the more difficult chunks
when they have some sentence context to help them.
In unlocking this sentence, for example,
a child who has gained skill in rearranging sentences
will not bog down on the introductory chunk of meaning
if the words are unfamiliar to him.

> Pressing his lithe body
> against the plastered wall,
> he listened
> and heard Nag and Nagaina
> whispering together
> outside in the moonlight.
>
> —"Rikki Tikki Tavi," *Sounds of Mystery*

Rather, he will skip down to the third chunk,
he listened,
which offers a more direct entry into the sentence.
Certain children have intuitively done this
as the natural way for making a go of a book,
until narrow reading instruction cuts them off
from this sensible, linguistically sound way
for handling complex print,
and instead teaches them to stop dead in their tracks
while they try to sound out each word
in that complicated first chunk of meaning.

Throughout *Sounds of Language* you will find
type arranged in unique and intriguing patterns—
part of our scheme to invite children
to use chunks of meaning to unlock
the linguistic puzzle.

I LOVE YOU, BIG WORLD. I wish I could call you And tell you a secret: That I love you, World... I love you, World...

by *Paul Wollner*

AGE 7

UNITED STATES

—from *Sounds of a Powwow*

8 FIGURING OUT HOW WORDS WORK

In basal reading programs and phonics programs
children spend their waking hours
considering the various ways in which words work.
In fact, in most of these programs
the word seems to be the only unit of language
worth studying.
Children learn about beginnings of words
and ends of words and middles of words.
They learn about special endings such as inflected endings.
They learn how the various letters behave in words.
And all of this they learn (or try to learn)
in line with prescriptive lesson plans
laid out in the teacher's guide.
When it is beginning consonant season,
heaven help the child who is good at looking at ends of words.
In some programs, children have to wait to beginning second grade
to even know that words have middles,
because that is when the teacher's guide
presents medial vowels.
Moreover, the methods used in teaching about words
are largely prescriptive.
Children are not invited to experiment with words
and come up with their own generalizations.
They are asked to memorize other people's generalizations
about what happens when two vowels go walking,
even though we all know that the first one does the talking
only when it feels in the mood.

You may or may not be using one of these programs
in your classroom.
Whether you do or not,
you and your children still need
the kind of spontaneous word analysis time
that is made possible with the *Sounds of Language* program.

In the same way that the children figure out
how stories and poems and sentences work
by experimenting with structures and verbalizing their discoveries,
children need to use their self-selected ways
for figuring out how words work.

Sometimes your open-ended questioning after reading a story or poem
will trigger discussions
which help children figure out how words pattern.
Supposing you have read:

One Misty, Moisty Morning

When cloudy was the weather,

I chanced to meet an old man

Clothed all in leather.

He began to compliment

And I began to grin:

"How do you do?"

And "How do you do?"

And "How do you do?" again.

—from *Sounds of Numbers*

After you and the children have thoroughly enjoyed the poem
through oral and various arrangements of choral reading
and after the children are using books
so their eyes are seeing the same patterns that their ears are hearing,
you might ask:

> *Children, what do you see interesting*
> *about those two words* misty *and* moisty?

Accept any observations the children care to make.

If Henry tells you that they both **Misty, Moisty**
have *y* at the end,
don't become ill at ease
if you are only studying beginning consonants
in your other reading program.
Some children are better at observing the ends of words
than they are at observing the beginnings of words
when they first start looking at print.
If these children learn
that nice boys don't look at the ends of words
simply because a prescriptive phonics program
is insisting on beginning sounds,
they begin to feel that there is something wrong
about them and reading
and they learn not to focus on the patterns of words
and certainly not to report their observations
if they do take a look.
How much better to praise Henry
for his accurate observation.

> *Henry, you're so great*
> *at looking at the ends of words.*
> *Perhaps you can find something else interesting*
> *about the way* misty *and* moisty *end.*

By now Henry is with you full force.
And on the heels of his success
in looking at the ends of words,
he can probably also be invited
to take a look at the beginnings of the two words.
By now some child will probably report to you,

> *Look.* **Moisty** *is bigger in the middle.*

Now the children have come face-to-face
with an interesting generalization about the ways words work.
They have beginnings and endings and middles.

inggallopinggallopinggallopinggallopinggallopingga
ggallopinggallopinggallopinggallopinggallopinggallo
gallopinggallopinggallopinggallopinggallopinggallop

The generalization has meaning
because in the first place,
they were scrutinizing the printed form
of two words that entered their linguistic storehouses
through the heat and drama of read-aloud.
They are not just cold words on a workbook page.
They are words the children truly own.
The generalization also has meaning
because the children were able to sneak up on it,
as it were,
knowing it intuitively from their experiences
with oral language
and gradually verbalizing this facet
of the shape of words they are seeing in print.

One useful question
for getting this kind of discussion going is simply:

> *Children, what do you see interesting*
> *about the words on this page?*

As the children report observations
about how letters fall next to one another in words
you will have an interesting diagnostic
of who the individual children are as word-unlockers.
The child who reports seeing three words
that "all have two t's in the middle"
is telling you that he sees letter patterns in words.
The child who reports a word
"that looks just like a fish,"
may be telling you that he is one of those children
who goes into reading by seeing pictures in words
rather than spelling patterns.
How exciting!

—from a word design from *Sounds of a Distant Drum*

nggallopinggallopinggallopinggallopinggallopinggallo
gallopinggallopinggallopinggallopinggallopinggallop
allopinggallopinggallopinggallopinggallopinggallopin

One productive activity
in helping primary children figure out how words work
(as well as how sentences work),
is to invite them to collect word cards
that they especially want.
This is markedly different from handing out
the same word cards to all children
with the requirement that they learn the word
as part of their basal reading program.
In this latter approach, it is the teacher who is reaching out,
trying to capture the child
and get him to learn the word selected by the teacher's guide.
When children ask for word cards of their own choosing,
they are the ones doing the reaching-out
and consequently the motivation comes from within themselves
rather than from the pressures of the outside world.
Children the nation over
demonstrated to us what they can be like
when they are invited to claim interesting words as their own.
The culture offered children the word

Supercalifragilisticexpialidocious

on the wings of a song.
We didn't tell the children they had to learn the word
before they were allowed to sing the song.
We didn't tell them that
if they were in the low reading group
we would give them a small, uninteresting word
to take the place of this complex, exciting word.
And the children responded to our freely given invitation.
It was so exciting going around the country
while "Mary Poppins" was in full swing.
The children demonstrated how they can behave
when their love of words is rewarded
by a truly worthwhile offering.
Not only could they read supercalifragilisticexpialidocious.
They could count the syllables and spell it backwards!

Words in the *Sounds of Language* reading program
are thought of as the personal possessions of each child.
At the end of reading a story or poem
you need only ask:

> *Did anyone hear a word
> you would like as your own?*

Once you give a child a word card
for each of his favorite words or phrases,
the fun begins!
Children will compare words.
They will swap with one another.
They will ask you for a blank card
to copy a friend's word.
They will arrange their word cards in patterns that

1) begin alike,
2) sound alike,
3) end alike.

They will create sentences on their desks.
Their favorite words are apt to appear
in their drawings and in their speech.

And you—think of the possibilities
for your involvement!
One bright, sunshiny morning you might announce:

> *Boys and girls,
> you'll never guess what I did last night.
> I sat up writing parts of sentences.
> When I hold one of these parts
> up in the air, if you have a word
> that will finish the sentence,
> hold it up.*

Suddenly your room will come alive
with thirty different sentences
as children hold up word cards to complete
a provocative sentence starter such as:

> *Someday I am going to kiss a* _____.

Cinderella

astronaut

skinny

afternoon

dinosaur

wagon   dragon

magician

musician

piccolo player

scientific

horse face

Another day you might suggest:

> *Children, do you know what let's do today?*
> *Let's put one rubber band*
> *around the word cards you do recognize*
> *and one around the words you don't.*
> *Then supposing you choose*
> *one unknown word each day*
> *to work on and change over to your known words.*

On other days the children can arrange their words alphabetically,
can group them with rubber bands
as naming words, action words, and describing words.
You can tell from this discussion,
that giving children word cards
is not the end,
but rather the beginning of a whole host
of language encounters
that help children claim the glory and workings of words.
Although it is true that filling out word cards
demands effort on your part,
you will find yourself basking in the rich rewards.
How exciting to have children ask for and value new words,
and through innate curiosity about things they value,
to analyze these words down to their most unique characteristic.
By the way, if you think alphabetizing
is the preferred way for arranging and filing word cards,
you may want to listen to your children.
Children have been known to make arrangements of

> exciting words,
> > letter writing words,
> story writing words,
> > hard words,
> easy words,
> > and even last week's words.

Interestingly enough, when children themselves
decide on methods of categorizing and filing,
they know exactly where to look for the word they need.

Those of you who teach older boys and girls
may be wondering how you can offer
the joy and productivity of word cards.
Actually, older boys and girls
have been known to do this same kind
of self-selected word collecting
with various kinds of word lists in their notebooks.
A boy who keeps a list of describing words worth using
when you want to indicate whether you're for or against a team,
is more highly motivated
than the boy who is idly writing sentences
using a list of *today's new words.*
Throughout the *Sounds of Language* program,
children are helped to analyze
the printed characteristics of words.
Surprisingly enough,
the most useful investigation
does not necessarily focus on beginnings and endings and middles.
In terms of a child's natural way for moving into print,
the first step in word analysis
is to hear and say the word orally
and count the number of syllables.
The sound of a word is its most unique characteristic
and it tends to be reflected in the printed symbol.
Let's pronounce and take a look at the word *station:*

The workmen
are going to build
a new police station here.

sta/tion

Ear and eye work comfortably together
in the word *station.*
It is easy to hear that there are two parts.
What are the useful steps to take in word analysis?

First: *"Let's listen to the word* station, *Chuck.*
How many sounds do you hear?"

Second: *"Look at the word, Chuck. (sta/tion)*
I am writing it on the chalkboard the way you say it."

Third: *"Now read the sentence in which you found the word, Chuck.*
Do you hear two sounds in station*?"*

Fourth: *You move from here to any next sensible step.*
It might be to look
at that intriguing tion *syllable*

"Let's look at some other two-syllable words
that look something like the word station.

sta	**tion**
na	**tion**
no	**tion**

Who knows where you go from here?
It might be to other two-syllable words
in the story, "The House Biter."
It might be to the wonderful
four-syllable word *education*
or to the intriguing *stationary*
that carries the original word *station.*

But whatever sequence you take,
you must be secure in the fact
that you can follow your own hunches
and your own common sense
in response to clues given by the children.
Children love to analyze a word they have discovered
in the context of a meaningful language pattern.
Let's not fool ourselves into believing
that there is only one sequence in word analysis.
Individual children and teachers have their own continuities
and this program invites you to respect these differences.

Then along came ÞUTTLEFiSʰ

9 FIGURING OUT HOW PRINT WORKS

When a child looks at a page of print,
something dynamic must happen if we hope for him to become
an intelligent, self-motivated reader.
Oh, we can force him to read as we do in many programs,
but unless he himself elects to explore the page of print
in an effort to make sense out of it,
we can safely assume
that he is not learning much about reading.
The traditional answer to this
has been simply to write stories with scaled vocabulary
so that a child's eyes will immediately see familiar words,
but there is much more
that can encourage a child to explore a page of print
than the sighting of familiar words.

You will discover that on many pages of *Sounds of Language* readers,
the type swells, lurches, screams, whispers,
undulates, turns somersaults,
and even subsides in pictorial and narrative context.

It swam around, and around, and around, and around, and around, and around, and around, and around, and around, and around. It looked at the worm on the pin. It waggled its tail.

FOOD, GLORIOUS FOOD! HOT SAUSAGE & MUSTARD!

—from *Sounds of a Distant Drum*

Having type behave in intriguing ways is not foreign to children.
We adults have grown accustomed to schoolbooks
where the same size and style of type
move relentlessly from left to right, page after page,
and it is easy to forget that today's children are encountering
imaginative and flamboyant uses of type on TV,
in magazine advertising
and even on their cereal boxes.

Watch children's faces as they follow the dancing type
in *"Ten Little Indians"* from *Sounds I Remember.*
Notice how intently their eyes move with the type
and how their spirits buoy with the playful design.
In impressive ways these young children are learning
the most basic characteristic of type—
it moves from one place to another.

The sad fact is,
most of the early reading programs,
with their insistence on a rigid left-to-right
non-varying pattern of print,
actually cut children off from a fundamental cultural experience
which tells children that print is
a very versatile and exciting human invention
which to a large degree bends itself to the desires of the user.
Rules about beginning on the left and moving to the right
are not impressive invitations into the world of print.
It is a child's recognition that type moves,
a recognition that most easily comes
from pages where the movement is exaggerated,
and his determination to figure out the plan
back of the typographical puzzle
that motivate a child to make a go of reading.
Once he is caught up in the excitement
of following the movement of type as he reads,
he will himself come to the generalization
that for the most part in the English language,
type does move from left to right.

As you leaf through the *Sounds of Language* books,
you will discover that in addition to other
exciting typographical innovations,
the type generally is set in the pattern of spoken language,
just as the type in this essay
has been printed in facsimiles of oral language patterns.
Various methods have been used
to cause the reader to focus attention on selected words,

i   t relationships.
  m   n
    p   e
      o   r
     r   e
       t   h
        a
         n   n
           t ideas, and i

And now for a moment of frankness . . .
When you first looked at this series of books,
did you realize that it was for purposes
of helping children figure out how print works
that the books were designed as they are?
Children are curious about how print works,
just as they were curious about how spoken language works.
The *Sounds of Language* readers reward this curiosity
by helping children relate all that they know about spoken language
as they unravel the secrets of print
and make these secrets work for them.
You will want to help the children verbalize
their adventures with print in the *Sounds of Language* readers.

Children, can you see the shapes of those words
slurpy and glurpy? Take a close look.

—from *Sounds Around the Clock*

and I, Trotting to market with cheeses and pie, Trotting to
Oh Donkey take care. Hey la
la, Ho la, If no one should
stumble, we'll never get there,
market with cheeses and pie,
Hey la la, Ho la, My donkey
and I. Hey la la, Ho la, Oh Donkey
never get there, Hey la la, Ho la,
My donkey and I, We'll eat
those cheeses, And we'll
eat that pie, Hey la la, Ho la,
If no one should buy, we'll eat those cheeses.
If you should stumble, we'll
Hey la la, Ho la, My donkey
Hey la la, Ho la, My donkey

An old song, author
unknown.

Herman
Vic
painting by

—from *Sounds After Dark*

As the children pore over this especially designed page,
they are role-playing in exaggerated fashion
the fact that if a person studies the puzzle of a page of print
he will discover signals and patterns
that help him decode what he is encountering.

In a similar way
when a child looks at the printed page of the old song above
and says, "I know where that song begins,"
he is showing that he has found enough clues
to get a start on unravelling the puzzle.
Which clues worked for him?
Was it the capital letter? Starting on the left?
The space in the lower left-hand corner?
The actual clues he found do not matter as much as the fact
that he expects his search to be rewarded.

One indication that the children are beginning
to make typographical arrangements work for them
is their experimentation with intriguing arrangements
of words and letters and numbers in their own writing.
The more children can get the notion that written language
is an exciting and dependable puzzle
with multiple clues for the person who is reading,
the more confident and successful they will be
in their independent reading.

For the psychological advantages as well as for pure enjoyment,
from time to time write on the board
familiar sentences in reverse direction,
in scattered fields of letters,
in upright rocketing,
in straight downward plunges,
in crisscross fashion.
And even upside down and backwards.

Then watch the children delight
as they put all of their linguistic skills
into the decoding of the language.
It is dramatic experiences like these
that stand children in good stead
as they engage in the routine aspects of decoding.
Children will work at identifying initial consonants
or medial vowels or moving from left to right
with more personal determination and pleasure
when they see such activities
as part of the larger and more exciting process
of figuring out the puzzle of print.

10 DEVELOPING SKILL IN COMPREHENSION

Contrary to the view of many reading programs,
comprehension is not merely a matter
of the reader's proving that he has "read" the selection.

All too often this kind of proving simply means
listing main events, main characters, key words,
character traits, and snatches of figurative language.
Comprehension activities takes on true character
when they involve the reader or listener in such ways
that he comes to grips
with his and his colleagues' personal interpretations
in relation to the author's intended meanings.
If you care about this kind of comprehension,
much depends on the kind of questions you ask children.
For example, a question like

> *How far did John walk?*

has only one possible answer to children
who have just read that John walked six miles.
Even if a child gives the "correct" answer,
what has he actually gained from this "educative process"?
As a matter of fact, the first child who gives the answer
closes the discussion.
The "educative process" comes to a close.
There is nowhere else the discussion could possibly go.
And how smart some children are in knowing
which children in the group will give the *correct answers* first!
Many simply do not expect to participate
in unimaginative rituals of this kind,
and gladly play the role of passive observers
because the situation structures such roles.

Think, on the other hand, what happens to children
if the teacher accepts the fact
that she doesn't have to make the children prove
that they have read the story threadbare,
and, therefore, can ask intriguing comprehension questions,
such as,

> Children, the story says John walked six miles.
> How far is six miles?

Every child now—even those who read less well than others—
views himself as an active participant in the discussion
and will gladly contribute his thoughts and feelings,
knowing that the purpose is to examine and probe personal meanings.

You may want to ask yourself if your questions
are the kind that stimulate thoughtful discussions
by which each reader can evaluate the meanings
he gleaned from and brought to the story.
Nothing is more exciting, more conducive to learning,
than to participate in a cross-fire of opinions and ideas
generated by a common experience, such as story meanings.
Here are some examples of questions
that will trigger off lively discussions
that will contribute to children's comprehension of the world
in which they live:

> How long is a person young?

The story "Growing Up, Growing Older" says,

> John is now a young man.
> He is eighteen years old.

How easy and unrewarding it would be to ask:

> How old was John when he was a young man?

A child could answer 18 years old and be correct,
but what kind of thinking,
what kind of language usage,
what kind of mental and emotional involvements
does his answer promote?

The openness of a true comprehension question invites children
to put everything they know about life
(in this case, what constitutes being young or old)
into their answer.
It also invites all children to participate in the discussion,
not only he who happens to speak first.
And make no mistake!
When you ask children how long a person is young,
you are going to get an array of life-related answers.
Many a child feels old at six,
and anyone old enough to go to college is positively antiquated.

Your comprehension questions about a story
will trigger off a whole hierarchy of meanings
ranging from gross understanding to precise verbalizing,
from a simple restatement of story meanings
to a complex conjecture about the whole realm of living.

Annotated in *Sounds of Laughter* for the consideration of both you
and the children is the question:

> *Is it hard not to speak in anger*
> *when your heart is filled with anger?*

The children have just been reading
the story of an Indian boy and his grandfather
and they have heard the grandfather advise the boy
not to speak in anger.
But the concern of the moment is not the grandfather's advice.
The concern is the feelings of the alive children in your classroom
who are encountering this advice.
We must not assume that comprehension can be measured
only in terms of "correct" answers to tight little questions.
The important thing is,
each child is pitting his own meanings against the author's
and gradually coming to know what the story means to him.
The cross-pollenation that occurs
in such discussions
also invites children to question their own meanings
and even to organize new meanings.

Here are some examples of questions
that should trigger lively discussions
that will both focus the literary experience
and contribute to children's comprehension of human behavior.

A) *Did you ever stop to think that there could be
such a thing as a bird that doesn't fly?
What makes a bird a bird anyway?*
"At Home on the Ice," *Sounds of a Hound Dog*

B) *If Bill held an after-school job for which he was paid a salary,
would he, after finding the trapped duck, have
ignored the reporting-in time, just as he did
when it was time to report in to his mother at dark?
Would you?* "The Web of Winter," *Sounds of Mystery*

C) *Do you like Mr. Lincoln better with or without a beard?
Why?* "A Vote for a Beard," *Sounds of a Young Hunter*

D) *Well, children, what do you think
of a free-wheeling literary-artistic-dramatic-boisterous
story like this?*
"How Old Stormalong Captured Mocha Dick," *Sounds of a Distant Drum*

Another insightful way of getting into
a full-blown discussion of story meanings
is to ask questions that relate to the author or artist's techniques
of putting a story or a picture together.

A) *A comparison of the descriptive line in "Facts About
Angry Bears"
with the dramatic story line in "Little Balser and the
Big Bear"
(or any other comparison of a factual article
with a story with a strong plot), for example,
will reveal much of children's understanding of the
selections,
although, ostensibly, they are discussing literary
structure.*—from *Sounds of a Young Hunter*

B) *What has the artist done in this picture to convey to you that this is a make-believe story?*
   "The Battle of the Furniture," *Sounds Jubilee*

C) *What clues do you get from the title and the illustrations as to what kind of reading you will find in this selection?*
   "The Birth and Growth of a Tree," *Sounds of a Distant Drum*

Enough comprehension questions have been annotated
throughout this program
to give you the feel of framing open-ended questions
that promote a depth of comprehension and feelings of self-respect.
Once you have experienced
the dynamics of a vital group discussion,
in contrast to a boring kind of question-answer ritual,
you will be well on your way to becoming that kind of teacher
whom children remember and revere.
The art of good teaching has deep roots
in the ability to motivate meaningful discussions.
Of course, post reading discussions are not the only way
for children to organize their reading meanings.
When the fourth grade teacher reads

> Giant Thunder striding home
>
> wonders if his supper's done.
>
> *'Hag wife, Hag wife, bring me my bones!'*
>
> > *'They are not done,'* the old hag moans.
>
> *'Not done? not done?'* the giant roars
>
> and heaves his old wife out of doors.

and Bill blurts out *"Sounds just like my father!"*
it is not necessary to ask a lot of tight little questions
about who came striding home and what wasn't done.
Bill's comprehension is proved in his spontaneous response
and the laughter of his classmates
is ample proof that Bill's comprehension is shared.

When the kindergarten teacher opens to the title page
of an honest-to-goodness spooky book
and Therese promptly gets up from her place
at the teacher's feet
and moves as far away from the book as possible
while still remaining in hearing range,
there is little doubt but that Therese understands
the mood of the story.
And as the story progresses
and Therese keeps moving back and forth—
now near the book, now far away—
she is using her entire body
to express her comprehension of the story.
Six-year-old Brenda's spontaneous response to A. A. Milne's line

So I think I'll be six now for ever and ever.

—from *Sounds Around the Clock*

needs no explanation.

I do not want to be six
for ever because I want to be
a nurse because I want to help
people and a whole gob of
people
will say thank you. Brenda

—1st Grade, J. J. Ingalls School, Kansas City, Kansas

Children are bubbling with spontaneous responses
to stories and poems until they learn
that there is only one thing that happens
after reading a story:
the teacher asks questions.
If your children do not seem to respond spontaneously
and you have a notion it is because
they are in this other habit of thinking about story response,
you may have to be the one in your class who responds
spontaneously to a story
in order to get the whole spontaneous,
personalized reaction-thing going.
After reading about John and his six mile walk,
for example, if you slap yourself on the thigh
and exclaim

> *WOW! What an idiot!*

and in other ways role-play the fact
that this kind of responding is a legitimate way
for showing comprehension,
the children will soon pick up the invitation
and reading time will take on more life.

And of course you are aware
that painting and dancing and creative dramatics
are also productive ways
for organizing personal meanings
brought into play by a story or poem or article.

One last thought about comprehension.
You may be interested to reread our discussion
FIGURING OUT HOW STORIES AND POEMS WORK, page 24.
And **FIGURING OUT HOW SENTENCES WORK**, page 56.
In both of these teaching strategies
are numerous suggestions
of times when the structure of a story or poem or sentence
deeply influences the meaning.
Those of us who study language in human affairs
can only conclude that structure is itself
one expression of meaning.

The post-reading discussions in *Sounds of Language*
that are triggered off by the open-ended comprehension questions
and by certain language-analysis questions

A) put each child in touch with his own thoughts and
feelings that have been generated by the reading,

B) put him in touch with the feelings and thoughts
of other children who supposedly shared an "identical"
reading experience, and

C) help him verbalize his growing insights
into the workings of language, both in oral and written
form.

The child's self-expressions, therefore, have a rare dynamic quality
as he searches for verbal ways to express the inner growth
that his reading occasioned.
Every speaking skill he employs,
everything from sentence patterns to figures of speech,
is influenced by the integrity of his speaking situation.
His *preciseness* in self-expression, therefore,
actually is preciseness in making language work to express
and thereby validate his own personality.

11 LINKING WRITING TO READING

In *Sounds of Language* children are helped
to develop writing skills
in the same naturalistic, linguistically sound ways
that they learn to read.
Just as kindergarteners and young first graders
latch on to highly structured rhymes and stories
and role-play themselves as readers,
these same young children begin innovating
on the author's pattern and role-play themselves as writers.

Hello! My name is Pamela, K.
I am a maker of costumes.
I make funny costumes and scary
costumes. These are the
costumes I make.

—2nd Grade, J. J. Ingalls School
Kansas City, Kansas

Gradually they learn to use their *Sounds of Language* books
as resource books for personal writing.
They know that these books are crammed
with story patterns and rhyme schemes and sentence patterns
that are theirs for the asking.
They also know that they have the practical know-how,
transforming sentences, for example,
for taking an author's structure
and hanging their own thoughts on it.

As one young child exultantly declared
after borrowing the literary structure
and sentence patterns of "The Billy Goats Gruff"
to successfully write his own story about three skunks
who encountered a troll on their way to eat garbage:

I only needed three new words
for my whole story—
    skunk
    and garbage
    and smelly.
I almost needed the word stinked
so I could say
the skunk stinked the troll,
but I remembered
you gave me the word skunk
and I could use that to say
the skunk skunked *him.*

—from Mueller School, second grade, Wichita, Kansas

Once children become accustomed to using their reader this way,
you will be amazed by both the quality and quantity
of their writing.
Moreover, you will have a solution to the nagging problem
of what kinds of "seat work" to provide the rest of the class
while you are busy with a few children.

12 CULTIVATING LITERARY AND ESTHETIC APPRECIATION

The content of the *Sounds of Language* readers
is specifically planned to place literary appreciation
at the heart of the reading program.
From the very first day of first grade
throughout the entire elementary school experience,
children using *Sounds of Language* readers
will be living in the midst of a gallery of contemporary art
and in a climate of literary appreciation
that sensitize their responses and imprint their memories
with high idealism and soul-stirring emotions.

Esthetic response can only be nurtured.
It cannot be taught.
By a wide and continuing exposure
to stories, poems, art, photos, and language
that possess some pretension to taste,
children will begin to know what they do and do not like.
Knowing what one does not like
is equally important as knowing what one enjoys.
Whatever else, a child's response must be self-selected,
and it must be sincere.
We teachers need to learn how to live with children's responses
which move against the grain of our own preferences
and which reveal pleasure in the mundane.
Many children, for example, will necessarily go
through a long period of literary exposure
before they are apt to sense the worthwhileness
of Emily Dickinson's poem "Autumn"
as compared to the joy they found in their favorite comics.

Be assured that those pleasurable times of the day
when you read aloud to children
are all a part of a program in literary and esthetic appreciation,
as well as a part of the reading program.

One especially productive technique
for helping children make these kinds of value judgments
comes about through an adaptation of Sidney Simon's value line
suggested in the drawing on the opposite page.
Simply list a few of the stories and/or poems and/or articles
the children have been reading
and suggest that they rate each one
by placing it in a self-selected spot
on their own copy of the value line.
In order to help the children understand
that the value line is not an instrument
for placing one selection at the low end of the line,
another at the high end,
and the rest at equal intervals along the line,
you might want to engage them in conversation
about their use of the line.
Help them understand that the value line
does not only apply to the seven stories
they are rating at this time.
The value line has places for all the stories
they have or ever will read.
The seven stories they are rating today
might all fall at the middle or top of the line.
Or they might scatter up and down the line.
You see, the value line is actually part of each of us.
It is man's way
for placing a value on things he encounters in life.
The value line might be used to rate happenings
or foods or school subjects or teachers or movies, etc.
The important thing to remember is—
there is no special ruler to measure the experiences of such stories, etc.
and to place them on the value line.
It is a person's response from his value
that places them one place or another on the value line.

Don't try to tell the children all about the line
at one sitting.
Put the line on the board
and start using it informally,

asking the children for suggestions
as to where some of the stories might fall.
As you talk together and the children differ
about certain ratings,
they will come to understand how the line works.
After a few minutes, suggest that they draw their own lines
and place the seven stories where they want them.

1) *House Afire!*

2) *When Christmas Comes*

3) *The Grandmother*

4) *The Ax*

5) *The Mice Who Loved Words*

6) *The First Schlmiel*

7) *Every Man Heart Lay Down*

—selections from *Sounds Jubilee*

LOW   MID   HIGH

Once the children have placed the stories somewhere on the line,
the fun begins.
Invite the children to meet as a group
to discuss their various placements.
How your classroom will ring with developing values
as the children explain and even defend
their various designations on the line!
And what a basic learning for the children
when they discover that three people can read the very same story
and come up with highly different evaluations—
all of which can be defended.
They might even deduce that if three different teachers
rather than just one gave them report card grades,
they would come up with differing marks.
What a nice blow to the righteousness of report card grades!

13 DEVELOPING SENSITIVITY TO THE THREE LEVELS OF LANGUAGE

Sounds of Language rejects the notion of "right" and "wrong"
in judging a child's language performance.
We recognize, instead, that there are three levels of language
that every child has a right
to experiment with, enjoy, and claim as his own.

A) Home-Rooted Language

The first level of language,
indigenous to the child's life itself,
is his *home-rooted (in-group) language*.
This language may or may not be grammatically correct.
It is the language he inherited from his family,
the language that is native to his soul
and sounds best to his ear.
This language may or may not feed comfortably
into the classroom,
but if we want our classrooms to be language laboratories
where a child feels free to experiment
with new linguistic patterns,
we must first of all respect the language he brings to school.
Both you and the children may be surprised to see
the number of selections in *Sounds of Language*
that are written in *home-rooted language*.
This can help both you and the children
better respect vernacular for its beauty
and for its direct communicative impact.
Isn't it fortunate that folklore
has helped us keep the richness of home-rooted language
in the bloodstream of our language heritage!

A copperhead snake made for me
one day when I was hoein' my corn.
Happened I saw him in time,
and I lit into him with the hoe.

He thrashed around,
bit the hoe-handle a couple of times,
but I fin'lly killed him.
Hung him on the fence.
Went on back to work,

—from "The Snakebit Hoe-handle," Sounds of a Young Hunter

For a picture of what linguistic heights
young children can reach
when their home-rooted language is respected,
see the dictated story from a young primary child
on the next page.
Obviously someone had read "The Billy Goats Gruff"
to this child, and just as obviously,
the child stored the basic structure of the story
in his linguistic storehouse.
Notice how faithful he is to the fact
that this is a story organized around a problem.
How faithful he is to the repetition in the episodes!
How faithful he is to the solving of the problem!
If the school had *made* him feel uncomfortable about his language,
he would have "dried up" and looked like one of those "children
without language"
we hear so much about.
We ourselves wonder if it is so much a matter
of "children without language"
as it is a matter of children who have been asked in effect
to check their home-rooted language outside the classroom door.

Them all going up to the grass where you eat and the mean old troll said "Who walkin' on my bridge?" I comin' up to eat you and little Billy Goat said "Don't eat me. Wait for my next brother to come.

So da troll said O.K. I will wait. So he waited and the next brother comed and the big old troll said who walkin on my bridge. Me, next billy goat Gruff. Wait don't eat me wait.

Then boomp boomp I comin up to eat you. So he did. He tossed the mean old troll up to the sky and eat him all up.

B) Public Language

The second level of language is *public language*.
This is the corps of language ways
that society uses to carry on its organized life.
It is the grammatically correct language that facilitates
broad and precise communication with the English-speaking community.
When standards of "right" and "wrong" are used
to evaluate language (heaven forbid!)
public language is the form that is said to be "right."
Public language should not be made available to children,
on the basis of "right" and "wrong,"
but rather as one of three ways to express themselves.

Different situations call for different kinds of language.
Just as public language works best in some situations,
so does home-rooted language in others.
When a child knows that he has a choice in language usage,
public language for him gains intrigue and respect.
Many articles and essays in *Sounds of Language* are written
in public language
to help children appreciate its direct, uncluttered, and practical
effectiveness.

Most of the Indian tribes
of the early American frontier
lived by hunting buffalo
and other animals.
These tribes were wanderers.
They were good hunters
and fierce warriors.

—from *Sounds of a Distant Drum*

Westfield, Chautauque Co NY
Oct 15, 1860
Hon A B Lincoln
Dear Sir
My father has just come from
the fair and brought home
your picture and mr. Hamlin's.

—from *Sounds of a Young Hunter*

The children may be interested in discussing
why Grace Bedell chose public language
when writing her letter to Abraham Lincoln.
This can lead to a discussion
of whether certain home-rooted expressions
might be appropriate in a letter to a best friend, to a stranger.
These discussions of language choices
give children feelings of power and pleasure
about themselves as language users.

C) Life-Lifting Language

Sing hey! Sing hey!
For Christmas Day
Twine mistletoe and holly
For friendship glows
In winter snows,
And so let's all be jolly.

— an old rhyme from *Sounds of a Young Hunter*

The third level of language is *life-lifting (literary) language.*
It is any bit or unit of language,
such as a story or poem or expression,
that is so memorable that it tends
to impress itself indelibly on the mind
and thereby become part of the culture's cherished language ways.

In

December   *"Get*

autumn   *ready*

calls   *for a*

its   *winter*

warning,   *morning!"*

It has been our experience
that many children whose home-rooted language
does not open-end comfortably into the public language
take on the public forms more easily
through poetry and other literature
than they do in lessons on public language.

Peck

    peck

       peck

on the warm brown egg.

OUT comes a neck.

OUT comes a leg.

       How

          does

             a chick,

       who's not been about,

       discover the trick

       of how to get out?

—"Baby Chick" by Aileen Fisher,
Sounds of Numbers

Consider the language thrust that any child will receive
if, throughout his elementary school years,
he has such broad and continuous exposure to memorable language
that he intakes into his mind's treasury
twenty or more poems a year.
This experience in and of itself
provides a major bridge for any child
into the culture's language storehouse,
and, at the same time, fills his mind
with high idealism and humanistic feelings.
The pervasive use of choral reading and choral speaking
in *Sounds of Language* is geared to this end.

    Speak gently, Spring, and make no sudden sound;

    For in my windy valley, yesterday I found

    New-born foxes squirming on the ground—

        Speak gently.

—from "Four Little Foxes" by Lew Sarett,
Sounds of a Storyteller

Developing Sensitivity to the Three Levels of Language TE 125

All: We sing of thee, America,
Land we love, America,
Hear our song of Liberty,
Our country 'tis of thee.

Narrator: Our country 'tis of thee we sing,
land of New England meadows and southern cottonfields,
of county fairs, and ticker-tape parades,
barefoot boys with fishing rods
and Ladies' Day at the baseball park.
A land of steel,
and industry,
and invention
with a heart as big as Texas
and dreams as tall as the great Northwest.

All: But where did it all begin?
Who made it possible?

Narrator: Well, to start with
There was a man . . .

—from "Our Country 'Tis of Thee,"
Sounds of a Distant Drum

Moreover, the choral speaking and choral reading
that children continuously do as part of this reading program
help them develop an appetite for the life-lifting language of literature.
As children's ears begin to know the pleasures
of this kind of language and this kind of reading,
their whole disposition toward life as well as toward literature
is affected.

In developing attitudes of literary discrimination,
each child should be encouraged to keep a running list
of his five favorite stories and poems.
Whenever he wants to add a new favorite to his list,
he necessarily must decide which of his former favorites
must be removed.
Only by exercising his own judgment in these matters,
without interference by an over-anxious adult,
will he gradually refine his sensitivities to literary ways.

Paul Bunyan

A poem by Arthur S. Bourinot

Solo: HE CAME,
STRIDING
OVER THE MOUNTAIN,
THE MOON SLUNG ON HIS BACK,

All: LIKE A PACK,

Solo: A GREAT PINE
STUCK ON HIS SHOULDER
SWAYED AS HE WALKED,
AS HE TALKED
TO HIS BLUE OX
BABE;
A HUGE, LOOMING SHADOW
OF A MAN,

All: CLAD
IN A MACKINAW COAT,
HIS LOGGER'S SHIRT
OPEN AT THE THROAT

Solo: AND THE GREAT MANE OF HAIR

All: MATCHING,
MEETING

Solo: THE LOCKS OF NIGHT,
THE SMOKE FROM HIS CAULDRON PIPE
A CLOUD ON THE MOON,

All: AND HIS LAUGH
ROLLED THROUGH THE MOUNTAINS
LIKE THUNDER
ON A SUMMER NIGHT

Solo: WHILE THE LIGHTNING OF HIS SMILE

All: *Split* THE HEAVENS
ASUNDER.

—from *Sounds of a Distant Drum*

Developing Sensitivity to the Three Levels of Language TE 127

14 DEVELOPING SENSITIVITY TO HUMANNESS

Often in classroom teaching
we become so preoccupied with "skill development"
that we tend to forget that the primary purpose of teaching
is to help children claim kinship with man's humanity.
As you use the *Sounds of Language* selections
to create a spiritual setting in your classroom
that inculcates and fosters feelings of individual worth
and high idealism,
you can be assured that you are engaging
in humanly-useful language teaching and "skill development."

For it is *on the wings of words*
that man claims his identity with his culture.
We must help children find access to those words.

Can you imagine, without giving yourself over
to a feeling of great joy and accomplishment,
what will happen to children who for six years
during their elementary school reading experiences
feel the flow and depth of life-lifting language in their daily lives?

And if the *Sounds of Language* program
fulfills all of its expectations,
you and I and every concerned human being
who has dedicated himself to helping children learn
will have developed a camaraderie
that will change the course of language instruction in our schools
and make language truly available to children
in terms of their emerging human needs.